Unveiling the Art of Japanese Sashiko Stitching

Master Quilt Patterns Book with DIY Techniques

Maximus R Rios

THIS BOOK
BELONGS TO

....

....

Thanks ever so much to each of my cherished readers for investing the time to read this book!

I know you could have picked from many other books, but you chose this one. So, a big thanks for reading all the way to the end. If you enjoyed this book or received value from it, I'd like to ask you for a favor. Please take a few minutes to ***post an honest and heartfelt review on Amazon.com.*** Your support does make a difference and helps to benefit other people.

Thanks!

Table of Contents

SUMMARY	1
CHAPTER ONE	27
INTRODUCTION TO SASHIKO	27
CHAPTER TWO	46
HOW TO FOLLOW A SASHIKO PATTERN	47
CHAPTER THREE	54
THE MOST EFFECTIVE METHOD TO SASHIKO JOIN BIT BY BIT DIRECTIONS	54
CHAPTER FOUR	74
THE MOST EFFECTIVE METHOD TO SASHIKO STITCH, BEGINNING WITHOUT A KNOT, DECIDING STITCH LENGTH AND MAKING GOOD CORNERS	74
CHAPTER FIVE	89
WAYS TO TRANSFER A SASHIKO DESIGN ONTO FABRIC (5 OF 5 FEATHERWEIGHT INTERFACING METHOD)	89
CHAPTER SIX	97
STEP BY STEP INSTRUCTIONS TO SASHIKO STITCH, ORDER OF STITCHING, CARRYING THREADS OR NOT, AND THINGS TO AVOID	97
END	114

SUMMARY

Introduction to Sashiko: Sashiko is a traditional Japanese embroidery technique that has been practiced for centuries. It is a form of decorative stitching that is used to reinforce and repair fabric, as well as create beautiful patterns and designs. The word "sashiko" translates to "little stabs" or "little pierce" in Japanese, which accurately describes the technique used in this art form.

The origins of sashiko can be traced back to the Edo period in Japan, which lasted from the 17th to the 19th century. During this time, sashiko was primarily used as a way to mend and strengthen clothing, particularly among the working class. The technique involved using a simple running stitch to create geometric patterns on the fabric, which not only added strength but also enhanced the aesthetic appeal of the garment.

Sashiko was traditionally done using white thread on indigo-dyed fabric, creating a striking contrast that is characteristic of this art form. The indigo-dyed fabric, known as "aizome," was commonly used in Japan for its durability and resistance to fading. The white thread used in sashiko was typically made from cotton, which was readily available and easy to work with.

Over time, sashiko evolved from a practical mending technique to a decorative art form. The patterns and designs became more intricate and varied, reflecting the creativity and skill of the artisans. Today, sashiko is not only used for repairing and reinforcing fabric but also for creating unique and beautiful pieces of art.

One of the most distinctive features of sashiko is its repetitive and geometric patterns. These patterns are often inspired by nature, such as waves, mountains, and flowers. The stitches used in sashiko are typically evenly spaced and create a rhythmic and harmonious effect. The simplicity and precision of the stitches are what make sashiko so visually appealing.

In addition to its aesthetic appeal, sashiko also has practical benefits. The running stitches used in sashiko create a layer of reinforcement on the fabric, making it more durable and resistant to wear and tear. This is particularly useful for items such as clothing, bags, and quilts that are subjected to frequent use.

Sashiko has gained popularity outside of Japan in recent years, as people around the world have become more interested in traditional crafts and techniques. Many individuals and organizations now offer workshops and classes on sashiko, allowing people to learn and practice this art form themselves.

The Rich Heritage and Significance of Sashiko in Japanese Culture: Sashiko, a traditional form of Japanese embroidery, holds a rich heritage and significant cultural importance in Japan. This intricate stitching technique has been passed down through generations, serving both functional and decorative purposes. The word "sashiko" translates to "little stabs" or little pierce, which accurately describes the method of creating repetitive patterns by hand-sewing small stitches.

Originating in the Edo period (1603-1868), sashiko was initially used as a way to mend and reinforce clothing, particularly among the farming and fishing communities. The harsh conditions of these occupations necessitated durable garments, and sashiko provided a practical solution. By stitching layers of fabric together with a distinctive running stitch, the resulting clothing became more resistant to wear and tear.

This technique not only extended the lifespan of garments but also added a unique aesthetic appeal.

Beyond its functional purpose, sashiko also became a means of artistic expression. As the technique gained popularity, artisans began to incorporate intricate patterns and designs into their stitching. These patterns often drew inspiration from nature, such as waves, mountains, and flowers, reflecting the deep connection between the Japanese people and their natural surroundings. Sashiko embroidery became a way to infuse beauty and creativity into everyday objects, transforming them into works of art.

Sashiko's cultural significance extends beyond its practical and artistic aspects. It also holds symbolic meaning in Japanese culture. The act of stitching by hand is seen as a meditative practice, allowing the individual to focus their mind and find tranquility in the repetitive motion. This mindful approach to embroidery aligns with the principles of Zen Buddhism, which emphasizes being present in the moment and finding peace within oneself. Sashiko, therefore, serves as a form of mindfulness and self-reflection, connecting the practitioner to their inner self and the world around them.

In addition to its historical and cultural significance, sashiko has experienced a resurgence in popularity in recent years. Modern designers and artists have embraced this traditional technique, incorporating it into contemporary fashion and home decor. The timeless beauty of sashiko's geometric patterns and the craftsmanship involved in its creation have captivated people worldwide, making it a sought-after art form.

In conclusion, sashiko holds a deep-rooted heritage and cultural significance in Japanese society. From its humble beginnings as a practical mending technique to its evolution as a form of artistic expression and mindfulness practice, sashiko embodies the values and traditions of Japan. Its enduring popularity and

The Historical and Cultural Significance of Sashiko: Sashiko is a traditional Japanese embroidery technique that has a rich historical and cultural significance. The word sashiko translates to little stabs or little pierce in Japanese, which accurately describes the technique of stitching small, even stitches to create intricate patterns on fabric.

The origins of sashiko can be traced back to the Edo period in Japan, which lasted from the 17th to the 19th century. During this time, sashiko was primarily used as a form of functional embroidery to reinforce and repair clothing. The technique was particularly popular among the working class, as it allowed them to extend the lifespan of their garments and make them more durable.

Sashiko was not only practical but also served as a form of artistic expression. The patterns created through sashiko were often inspired by nature, such as waves, mountains, and flowers. These motifs were not only aesthetically pleasing but also held symbolic meanings. For example, the wave pattern represented strength and resilience, while the mountain pattern symbolized stability and endurance.

In addition to its functional and artistic aspects, sashiko also played a significant role in Japanese culture. It was often passed down through generations, with mothers teaching their daughters the technique as a way to preserve their heritage. Sashiko was also used to create traditional garments, such as kimono and haori jackets, which were worn during special occasions and ceremonies.

Over time, sashiko evolved from a practical embroidery technique to a form of decorative art. Today, it is widely appreciated and practiced not only in Japan but also around the world. Many artisans and enthusiasts have embraced sashiko as a way to connect with Japanese culture and express their creativity.

The popularity of sashiko has also led to the development of various sashiko-related products and workshops. Sashiko kits, which include pre-printed fabric and thread, allow individuals to easily try their hand at this traditional technique. Workshops and classes offer a more immersive experience, where participants can learn from experienced sashiko practitioners and gain a deeper understanding of the history and techniques involved.

In conclusion, sashiko holds a significant place in Japanese history and culture. Its origins as a functional embroidery technique have evolved into a form of artistic expression that is appreciated worldwide. The intricate patterns and symbolic meanings associated with sashiko reflect the values and traditions of Japanese society.

Traditional Sashiko Patterns and Their Meanings: Traditional Sashiko patterns are a significant aspect of Japanese culture and have been passed down through generations. These intricate designs hold deep meanings and are often used to embellish clothing, household items, and accessories. Sashiko, which translates to little stabs, refers to the stitching technique used to create these patterns.

One of the most well-known Sashiko patterns is the Asa-no-ha, or hemp leaf pattern. This design is characterized by a repeating geometric motif resembling the leaves of a hemp plant. The hemp leaf symbolizes growth, prosperity, and good fortune. It is often used in Sashiko to bring luck and abundance to the wearer or the household.

Another popular Sashiko pattern is the Shippou, or seven treasures pattern. This design features interlocking circles, each representing one of the seven treasures in Buddhism: gold, silver, lapis lazuli, crystal, agate, coral, and pearl. The Shippou pattern is believed to bring protection, wealth, and spiritual enlightenment. It is commonly used in Sashiko to adorn kimono sleeves and obi belts.

The Kaki-no-hana, or persimmon flower pattern, is another traditional Sashiko design with a rich meaning. The persimmon flower symbolizes longevity and good health. It is often stitched onto clothing or household items to bring blessings of vitality and well-being to the wearer or the home.

The Yabane, or arrow feather pattern, is a Sashiko design that represents protection and defense against evil spirits. The arrow feathers are believed to ward off negative energy and bring good luck. This pattern is commonly used in Sashiko to decorate garments worn during important ceremonies or events.

The Sayagata pattern is a geometric design consisting of interlocking swastikas or manji symbols. In Japanese culture, the swastika symbolizes eternity and good luck. The Sayagata pattern is often used in Sashiko to bring blessings of longevity, happiness, and prosperity.

These are just a few examples of the numerous traditional Sashiko patterns and their meanings. Each pattern holds its own significance and is carefully chosen to convey specific wishes or intentions. Whether it is for personal adornment or to enhance the beauty of everyday items, Sashiko patterns continue to be cherished and celebrated as a timeless art form in Japanese culture.

The Philosophy and Aesthetics Behind Sashiko: Sashiko is a traditional Japanese embroidery technique that has been practiced for centuries. It is characterized by its simple yet intricate stitching patterns, typically done with white thread on indigo-dyed fabric. While sashiko is often admired for its visual appeal, there is a deeper philosophy and aesthetic behind this art form.

At its core, sashiko embodies the principles of mindfulness, simplicity, and sustainability. The act of stitching requires a focused and meditative mindset, as each stitch is made with intention and precision. This mindfulness is reflected in the repetitive nature of the stitching patterns, which can be seen as a form of meditation. By engaging in sashiko, practitioners are encouraged to slow down, be present in the moment, and find tranquility in the rhythmic motion of the needle and thread.

Simplicity is another key aspect of sashiko. The designs are often composed of geometric shapes and lines, creating a minimalist aesthetic. This simplicity not only enhances the visual appeal of the embroidery, but also reflects the Japanese concept of less is more. Sashiko teaches us to appreciate the beauty in simplicity and to find elegance in the understated.

Furthermore, sashiko embodies the principles of sustainability and resourcefulness. Historically, sashiko was used as a way to mend and reinforce clothing, particularly in rural farming communities where resources were scarce. The stitching patterns were not only decorative, but also served a practical purpose of extending the life of garments.

This ethos of repurposing and making the most out of what we have is still relevant today, as sashiko encourages us to value and care for our belongings, rather than discarding them at the first sign of wear and tear.

In addition to its philosophical underpinnings, sashiko also has a distinct aesthetic that sets it apart from other embroidery techniques. The contrast between the white thread and indigo fabric creates a striking visual impact. The geometric patterns, such as the traditional asa-no-ha (hemp leaf) or shippou (seven treasures), add a sense of order and harmony to the design. The combination of these elements results in a timeless and elegant aesthetic that has captivated people around the world.

Overall, sashiko is more than just a decorative embroidery technique. It is a philosophy and aesthetic that encourages mindfulness, simplicity, and sustainability. Through its meditative stitching process, sashiko invites us to slow down and find peace in the present moment.

Introduction to Sashiko Needles, Thread, and Fabrics: Sashiko is a traditional Japanese embroidery technique that has been practiced for centuries. It involves stitching intricate patterns on fabric using a special type of needle, thread, and fabric. In this introduction, we will explore the different types of Sashiko needles, thread, and fabrics used in this art form.

Sashiko needles are unique in their design and purpose. They are longer and thicker than regular sewing needles, allowing for easier manipulation of the fabric. The needles have a sharp point, which helps in piercing through multiple layers of fabric without causing damage. They are also made of high-quality steel, ensuring durability and longevity. Sashiko needles come in various sizes, ranging from small to large, depending on the intricacy of the design and the thickness of the fabric being used.

Thread is another essential component of Sashiko embroidery. Traditionally, Sashiko thread is made from 100% cotton, which gives it strength and durability. The thread is usually thicker than regular sewing thread, allowing for more visible stitches. It comes in a wide range of colors, allowing artists to create vibrant and eye-catching designs. Sashiko thread is also known for its unique texture, which adds depth and dimension to the embroidered patterns.

When it comes to fabric, Sashiko embroidery is typically done on a sturdy and tightly woven fabric. The most commonly used fabric for Sashiko is called Kogin, which is a type of cotton fabric with a distinctive texture. Kogin fabric is known for its durability and ability to withstand the repeated stitching of Sashiko embroidery. Other fabrics that can be used for Sashiko include denim, linen, and even silk, depending on the desired effect and the artist's preference.

In addition to the needles, thread, and fabric, there are also various tools and accessories that can enhance the Sashiko embroidery experience. These include thimbles, embroidery hoops, and marking tools. Thimbles are used to protect the fingers while stitching, especially when working with thicker fabrics. Embroidery hoops help to keep the fabric taut and prevent it from shifting during the stitching process. Marking tools, such as water-soluble pens or chalk, are used to transfer the design onto the fabric before stitching.

In conclusion, Sashiko embroidery is a beautiful and intricate art form that requires specific tools and materials.

Choosing the Right Materials for Your Project of Sashiko: When it comes to choosing the right materials for your Sashiko project, there are several factors to consider. Sashiko is a traditional Japanese embroidery technique that involves stitching intricate patterns on fabric, typically using a running stitch. The materials you choose will greatly impact the final result of your project, so it's important to make informed decisions.

First and foremost, you'll need to select the appropriate fabric for your Sashiko project. Traditionally, Sashiko is done on a medium-weight, tightly woven fabric such as cotton or linen. These fabrics provide a stable base for the stitching and allow the patterns to stand out. It's important to choose a fabric that is easy to work with and can withstand the repeated stitching without fraying or distorting.

Next, you'll need to consider the thread you'll be using for your Sashiko project. Sashiko thread is typically a thick, cotton thread that is specifically designed for this embroidery technique. It's important to choose a thread that is strong and durable, as Sashiko involves a lot of stitching. The thread should also be colorfast, meaning it won't fade or bleed when washed. Traditional Sashiko thread comes in a range of colors, allowing you to create beautiful and intricate designs.

In addition to fabric and thread, you may also want to consider using a Sashiko needle. These needles are longer and thicker than regular sewing needles, making them ideal for the dense stitching involved in Sashiko. The larger eye of the needle also allows for easier threading of the thick Sashiko thread. Using a Sashiko needle will ensure that your stitches are even and consistent throughout your project.

Finally, you may want to consider using a Sashiko stencil or template to guide your stitching. These stencils are typically made of thin plastic or paper and feature pre-drawn patterns that you can follow. Using a stencil can help you achieve precise and uniform stitches, especially if you're new to Sashiko. They can also save you time and effort in designing your own patterns.

In conclusion, choosing the right materials for your Sashiko project is crucial for achieving the desired result. Consider the fabric, thread, needle, and any additional tools such as stencils that will help you create beautiful and intricate designs. By making informed decisions about your materials, you'll be well on your way to creating stunning Sashiko embroidery.

Setting Up Your Sashiko Workspace: Setting up your Sashiko workspace is an essential step in ensuring a smooth and enjoyable stitching experience. By creating a dedicated space for your Sashiko projects, you can maximize your productivity and focus on the intricate details of this beautiful Japanese embroidery technique.

First and foremost, you'll need a sturdy and spacious work surface. A large table or desk is ideal, as it provides ample room for your fabric, thread, and other necessary tools. Make sure the surface is clean and free from any debris that could potentially interfere with your stitching.

Next, consider the lighting in your workspace. Sashiko requires precision and attention to detail, so it's crucial to have adequate lighting to see your stitches clearly. Natural light is best, so try to position your workspace near a window. If that's not possible, invest in a good quality desk lamp that provides bright, focused light.

Organizing your tools and materials is another important aspect of setting up your Sashiko workspace. Keep your threads, needles, thimbles, and other supplies within easy reach, so you don't have to constantly search for them while working on your project. Consider using small containers or trays to keep everything organized and easily accessible.

Having a comfortable chair is also essential, as Sashiko can be a time-consuming process. You'll want to ensure that you can sit for extended periods without discomfort or strain. Look for a chair with good back support and adjustable height options to find the most comfortable position for your stitching.

Additionally, consider the noise level in your workspace. Sashiko requires concentration and focus, so it's best to minimize any distractions or loud noises that could disrupt your stitching flow. If you live in a noisy environment, consider using noise-canceling headphones or playing soft, calming music to create a peaceful atmosphere.

Finally, don't forget to personalize your workspace to make it truly your own. Add decorative elements such as plants, artwork, or inspirational quotes that inspire and motivate you during your Sashiko journey. Creating a visually appealing and inviting space will enhance your overall stitching experience and make it more enjoyable.

In conclusion, setting up your Sashiko workspace involves creating a dedicated and organized area where you can focus on your stitching projects. By ensuring you have a sturdy work surface, proper lighting, organized tools, a comfortable chair, and a peaceful environment, you'll be well-equipped to embark on your Sashiko journey with ease and enjoyment.

The Fundamental Sashiko Stitch: The Fundamental Sashiko Stitch is a traditional Japanese embroidery technique that has been practiced for centuries. It is characterized by its simple yet intricate geometric patterns created by a series of running stitches. This stitch is not only visually appealing but also serves a functional purpose, as it reinforces the fabric and makes it more durable.

To create the Fundamental Sashiko Stitch, you will need a needle, thread, and a piece of fabric. Traditionally, a white or indigo-colored fabric is used, but you can experiment with different colors to create unique designs. The thread used is typically a thick cotton thread, known as Sashiko thread, which adds texture and depth to the stitch.

To begin, thread your needle with a length of Sashiko thread. It is recommended to use a longer thread to avoid frequent re-threading. Start by making a small knot at the end of the thread to secure it in place. Then, bring the needle up from the back of the fabric, leaving a small tail of thread on the wrong side.

Next, create your first stitch by inserting the needle back into the fabric, a short distance away from the starting point. The length of the stitch can vary depending on your desired design, but it is typically around 1/4 to 1/2 inch long. Ensure that the needle goes through both layers of fabric to create a secure stitch.

After completing the first stitch, bring the needle up again, this time a short distance away from the end of the previous stitch. Repeat this process, creating a series of parallel stitches that are evenly spaced. The spacing between the stitches can also vary depending on your design preferences, but it is typically around 1/4 to 1/2 inch apart.

As you continue stitching, you will notice that the thread starts to form a pattern on the fabric. This is where the beauty of Sashiko embroidery lies. The geometric patterns created by the running stitches can range from simple lines to intricate motifs, such as waves, flowers, or geometric shapes.

To finish the stitch, make a small knot at the end of the thread on the wrong side of the fabric. Trim any excess thread to create a neat and tidy finish. You can also secure the thread by weaving it through the back of the stitches before making the final knot.

The Fundamental Sashiko Stitch can be used to embellish various items, such as clothing, accessories, or home decor.

Techniques for Creating Consistent Stitches of Sashiko: Sashiko is a traditional Japanese embroidery technique that involves creating consistent stitches on fabric to create beautiful and intricate patterns. The art of Sashiko has been practiced for centuries and is known for its durability and strength. To achieve consistent stitches in Sashiko, there are several techniques that can be employed.

Firstly, it is important to choose the right fabric for Sashiko. Traditionally, Sashiko is done on a medium-weight, tightly woven fabric such as cotton or linen. This type of fabric allows for the stitches to be evenly spaced and creates a sturdy base for the embroidery. It is also important to ensure that the fabric is properly prepared before starting the stitching process. This can be done by washing and ironing the fabric to remove any wrinkles or creases that may affect the final result.

Next, it is crucial to use the right needle and thread for Sashiko. A long, thin needle with a sharp point is ideal for creating consistent stitches. The needle should be able to easily pass through the fabric without causing any damage or distortion. As for the thread, a thick, strong thread such as Sashiko thread or embroidery floss is recommended. This type of thread not only adds to the durability of the stitches but also enhances the overall appearance of the embroidery.

When it comes to creating consistent stitches in Sashiko, it is important to maintain a steady hand and a consistent stitch length. This can be achieved by using a thimble to protect your finger and provide stability while stitching. Additionally, it is helpful to mark the fabric with a grid or guidelines to ensure that the stitches are evenly spaced and aligned. This can be done using a water-soluble fabric marker or by creating small dots with a pencil or chalk.

Another technique that can be used to create consistent stitches in Sashiko is the use of a stitching template or stencil. These templates can be made from cardboard or plastic and are used to guide the needle and thread along a specific pattern or design. By following the template, the stitches can be evenly spaced and the overall design can be achieved with precision.

Lastly, practice and patience are key when it comes to creating consistent stitches in Sashiko. It takes time and effort to master the technique and achieve the desired results. It is important to start with simple patterns and gradually progress to more complex designs as your skills improve.

Practice Patterns for Beginners of Sashiko: Sashiko is a traditional Japanese embroidery technique that involves stitching decorative patterns on fabric. It is a popular craft that has been practiced for centuries and is known for its simplicity and elegance. If you are a beginner looking to learn and practice Sashiko, there are a few patterns that are perfect for starting out.

One of the most basic and commonly used patterns in Sashiko is the straight stitch pattern. This pattern involves stitching straight lines in a grid-like pattern on the fabric. It is a great pattern for beginners as it helps to develop the basic stitching technique and allows for easy practice. You can start by drawing a grid on your fabric using a fabric marker or pencil and then stitch along the lines using a Sashiko needle and thread. This pattern can be used to create beautiful designs on various items such as clothing, bags, and home decor.

Another popular pattern for beginners is the running stitch pattern. This pattern involves stitching parallel lines of small running stitches on the fabric. It is a versatile pattern that can be used to create various designs and motifs. To practice this pattern, you can start by drawing parallel lines on your fabric and then stitch along the lines using a running stitch. This pattern is great for creating borders, filling in larger areas, or adding texture to your Sashiko projects.

If you are looking for a more intricate pattern to challenge yourself, the interlocking circles pattern is a great choice. This pattern involves stitching overlapping circles on the fabric, creating a beautiful and intricate design. To practice this pattern, you can start by drawing circles of different sizes on your fabric and then stitch along the lines using a Sashiko needle and thread. This pattern requires more precision and attention to detail, making it a great pattern to improve your stitching skills.

As a beginner, it is important to start with simple patterns and gradually progress to more complex ones. This will help you develop your stitching technique and gain confidence in your Sashiko skills. It is also important to practice regularly and be patient with yourself as learning a new craft takes time and practice.

In addition to practicing different patterns, it is also helpful to learn about the history and cultural significance of Sashiko. Understanding the origins and traditions behind this craft can deepen your appreciation for it and inspire you to create meaningful and authentic Sashiko designs.

Overall, practicing Sashiko as a beginner can be a rewarding and enjoyable experience.

Integrating Sashiko Patterns into Larger Designs: Integrating Sashiko patterns into larger designs is a creative and visually appealing way to incorporate this traditional Japanese embroidery technique into various projects. Sashiko, which translates to little stabs, is characterized by its geometric patterns and repetitive stitching, traditionally done with white thread on indigo fabric.

When integrating Sashiko patterns into larger designs, it is important to consider the overall aesthetic and balance of the composition. The intricate and bold nature of Sashiko patterns can easily become overwhelming if not carefully incorporated into the design. Therefore, it is crucial to find the right balance between the Sashiko elements and the rest of the design.

One approach to integrating Sashiko patterns into larger designs is by using them as focal points or accents. For example, a Sashiko pattern can be placed strategically on a garment, such as a pocket or collar, to draw attention and add visual interest. This technique works particularly well when the rest of the design is kept simple and minimalistic, allowing the Sashiko pattern to shine.

Another way to incorporate Sashiko patterns into larger designs is by using them as borders or frames. This technique works especially well in textile design, where Sashiko patterns can be used to outline and enhance the edges of a larger pattern or motif. By using Sashiko as a border, the design gains a sense of structure and cohesion, while also showcasing the intricate stitching and geometric patterns.

In addition to using Sashiko patterns as focal points or borders, they can also be integrated into the overall design as repeating elements. This approach works well in surface design, such as wallpaper or fabric patterns, where the Sashiko motifs can be repeated in a grid-like formation. This creates a visually pleasing and harmonious design that showcases the beauty of Sashiko embroidery.

When integrating Sashiko patterns into larger designs, it is important to pay attention to color choices. Traditionally, Sashiko is done with white thread on indigo fabric, but there is no strict rule regarding color. Experimenting with different color combinations can add a modern twist to the traditional technique and allow for more versatility in design.

Overall, integrating Sashiko patterns into larger designs requires careful consideration of composition, balance, and color. By using Sashiko as focal points, borders, or repeating elements, designers can create visually stunning and unique designs that showcase the beauty and craftsmanship of this traditional Japanese embroidery technique.

Combining Different Sashiko Patterns: When it comes to combining different Sashiko patterns, the possibilities are endless. Sashiko, a traditional Japanese embroidery technique, involves stitching intricate patterns on fabric using a running stitch. This art form has been practiced for centuries and has evolved into a variety of patterns and designs.

To create a unique and visually appealing Sashiko piece, one can experiment with combining different patterns. This can be done by either stitching multiple patterns side by side or by incorporating elements from different patterns into a single design.

One approach to combining patterns is to stitch them side by side. This can create a visually striking effect, especially when contrasting patterns are used. For example, one could stitch a geometric pattern next to a floral pattern, or a wave pattern next to a checkered pattern. By carefully selecting patterns that complement each other, one can create a harmonious and balanced composition.

Another approach is to incorporate elements from different patterns into a single design. This can be done by selecting specific motifs or elements from different patterns and combining them in a creative way. For example, one could take a flower motif from one pattern and combine it with a wave motif from another pattern. This allows for a more personalized and unique design that showcases the individual's creativity and artistic vision.

When combining different Sashiko patterns, it is important to consider the overall composition and balance of the design. The patterns should complement each other and create a cohesive visual narrative. It is also important to pay attention to the scale and placement of the patterns to ensure that they work well together.

In addition to combining patterns, one can also experiment with different colors and thread combinations. Traditional Sashiko is typically done using white thread on an indigo fabric, but there is no rule that limits the use of color. By introducing different colors and thread combinations, one can add depth and dimension to the design, further enhancing its visual impact.

Combining different Sashiko patterns allows for endless creativity and exploration. It is a way to push the boundaries of traditional Sashiko and create unique and personalized pieces. Whether stitching side by side or incorporating elements from different patterns, the key is to experiment, have fun, and let your creativity guide you.

Exploring Variations and Personal Style in Sashiko: In the world of textile art, one technique that has gained popularity in recent years is Sashiko. Originating from Japan, Sashiko is a form of decorative stitching that was traditionally used to reinforce and repair garments. However, it has now evolved into a creative and expressive art form that allows individuals to explore variations and showcase their personal style.

When it comes to exploring variations in Sashiko, there are numerous possibilities to consider. One aspect that can be varied is the choice of thread color. Traditionally, Sashiko was done using white thread on indigo fabric, creating a striking contrast. However, modern practitioners have started experimenting with different thread colors, ranging from vibrant hues to subtle pastels. This variation in thread color can completely transform the look and feel of a Sashiko piece, allowing artists to create unique and personalized designs.

Another aspect that can be varied in Sashiko is the choice of stitch patterns. While there are traditional stitch patterns that have been passed down through generations, artists are encouraged to explore and create their own patterns. This allows for a wide range of possibilities, from simple geometric shapes to intricate floral motifs. By experimenting with different stitch patterns, artists can add their own personal touch to their Sashiko pieces, making them truly one-of-a-kind.

Furthermore, the choice of fabric can also contribute to the variation in Sashiko. While indigo fabric is the most commonly used material, artists can choose to work on different types of fabric, such as linen, cotton, or even silk. Each fabric has its own unique texture and drape, which can greatly influence the final outcome of the Sashiko piece. By selecting different fabrics, artists can create different effects and explore new possibilities in terms of texture and visual appeal.

In addition to exploring variations, Sashiko also allows individuals to showcase their personal style. Each artist has their own unique aesthetic and artistic vision, which can be reflected in their Sashiko work. Some artists may prefer bold and graphic designs, while others may lean towards delicate and intricate patterns. Some may choose to incorporate other elements, such as embroidery or appliqué, into their Sashiko pieces. The possibilities are endless, and Sashiko provides a platform for artists to express themselves and create pieces that truly reflect their personal style.

In conclusion, Sashiko offers a world of possibilities for individuals to explore variations and showcase their personal style. From experimenting with thread colors and stitch patterns to selecting different fabrics, artists

CHAPTER ONE
INTRODUCTION TO SASHIKO

A pattern in weaving: Sashiko sewing and noticeable repairing. This old Japanese art is not difficult to learn. It gives speedy outcomes and makes dazzling material pieces. In this instructional exercise we clarify the nuts and bolts you need to think about Sashiko sewing. We share our suggestions for Sashiko materials. [1]You will likewise discover bit by bit direction on the most proficient method to Sashiko line for amateurs.

Sashiko Origin

Sashiko began over a thousand years ago and has gain a lot popularity among Japanese peasants, martial artists, as well as even firefighters.

So get ready to spool up as we take a look back at sashiko's past millennium.

The Basics

Historically, sashiko was largely employed for garments, although the stitch has also been seen on curtains, bags, and other housewares. Sashiko is mostly done using white thread on fabrics, though the quantity of indigo depends on the region.

Stitch consistency is an important aspect of sashiko, and it can range from five to ten stitches per inch depending on the location. Of course, this necessitates a steady hand and a great deal of talent, which Japanese artists mastered mostly over the winter months. Other geographical differences included dye color and material, with wealthy rice-producing areas having darker garments because they could afford

had more access to imported cotton and wool, and could dip yarn in indigo vats many times. Stitching is done with two to three layers of a balanced-weave textile, which means that the warp and weft are of equal thickness.

Useful Applications

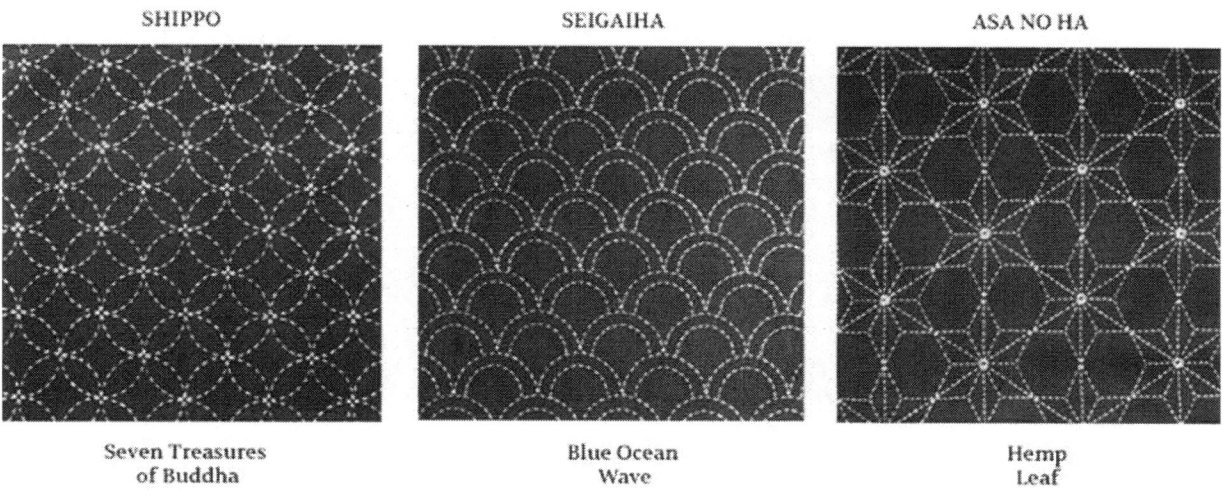

Most textiles had a much looser weave before the widespread availability of industrially woven fabrics. This made stitching the cloth much easier, and in some circumstances, the stitching actually made the garments warmer by warming the air trapped between the layers. The extra thread was also incredibly absorbent. This property was used by artists to absorb colours, and martial artists used it to absorb sweat.

For a long time, the martial arts Gi worn in Aikido has been woven in the sashiko manner. Sashiko was thick and strong, both of which were important in Aikido. It added durability to the clothes, wicking away sweat and providing padding, much to the relief of the wearer.

Because sashiko was mostly a home-art, the market for it wasn't particularly competitive, but the Kogin Kimonos were an exception. Kogin is a type of sashiko that is based on a diamond pattern that is repeated. Kogin kimonos were often constructed of rough hemp and were considered an important element of a woman's dowry. The five to seven kimonos given as dowry were also meant to be a barometer for the future bride's aptitude and mental acuity, thus they had to be meticulously embroidered.

The employment of sashiko by Japanese firefighters was perhaps the most astounding application of the technique. In Japanese cities, there were numerous ranks of firefighters, but The highly embroidered sashiko clothes depicted above were only worn by the common people.

The villagers started battling fires in 1718, and their uniform varied through time, but it was essentially a long coat made of three layers of cotton with sashiko stitching all over. The outfit was finished with quilted layers, socks, mittens, and even a hood. The entire heavy-duty cotton uniform was made to absorb as much as possible. Firefighters would douse themselves in water before entering a fire, allowing their clothing to absorb as much as possible. This can amount to as much as 70 pounds of water or more.

Repairing in the Modern Era

I had my doubts about sashiko repair on denim for a long time. I didn't understand what you were saying. However, after a few hours of research, it began to make sense. The Japanese geometric running stitch is both versatile and practical. For those of you without instant access to a darning machine, its convenience, resiliency, aesthetic appeal, and firefighting absorbency all combine to make it an extremely desirable repair technique.

Sashiko was usually made for personal or family use in the beginning, giving it a particular homespun character. No one's sashiko was the same as the next. Those exquisite stitches revealed whoever took the time to sew them, as well as their personal style and artistic vision.

Sashiko still straddles the border between form and utility, as it did in medieval Japan. Its undeniable elegance has made it a source of pride for Japanese (and now international) artisans, but it is, at its heart, a homegrown method of extending the life of and even improving regular old clothes.

Material Needed for Sashiko Projects

      1. Sashiko Needle

Depending on the scope of your project, you'll need either long or short Sashiko Needles.

Sashiko Needles, Short

Sashiko Needle is a Japanese needle that is used to make sashiko

You'll need either long or short Sashiko Needles, depending on the scope of your project.

Sashiko needles that are shorter

To produce straight lines, long Sashiko Needles are used. Because of the needle's length, it's easier to line a few lines at once.

Sashiko Fabric No. 2

In most cases, a dull blue evenweave texture from cloth or cotton that is heavier than broadcloth is used.

We recommend using evenweave textures rather than firmly woven plain textures. The evenweave texture's open structure makes it easier to weave the needle between the texture layers.

Two layers of texture can be used in the creation of garments. Multiple layers make your clothing hotter because warmth is trapped in the pockets of air you create when working on the plans.

You can get an environmentally friendly naval force blue cloth in our shop, which we love to use for Sashiko projects.

3. Sashiko Embroidery Thread

Sashiko is traditionally produced with a heavily twisted large weight cotton string. We prefer to use our 6 abandoned weaving floss because it is readily available in Europe. You can also use fine sew cotton or size 8 or 12 pearl cotton.

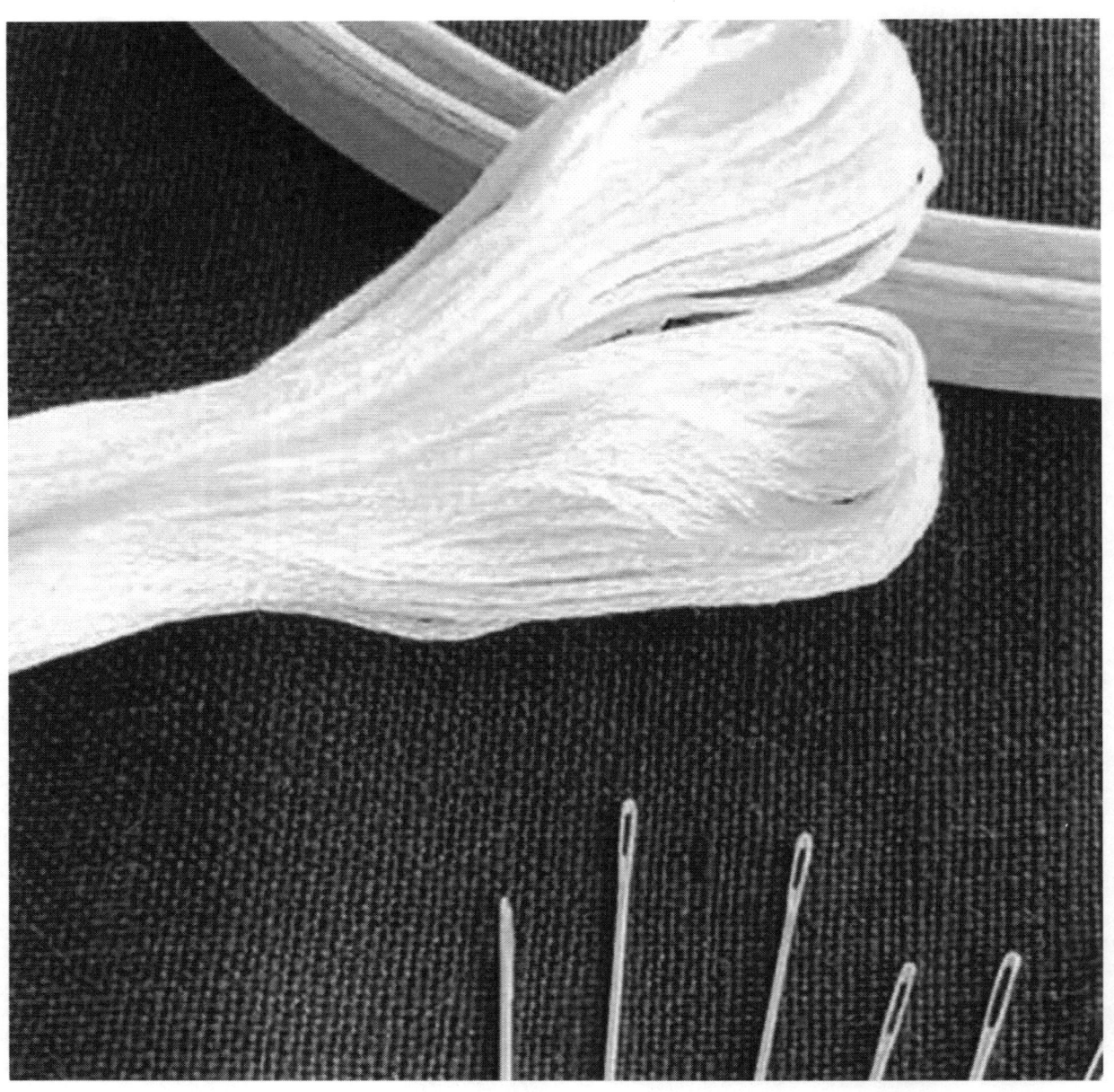

4. Sashiko Design

Nature is usually the source of inspiration for Sashiko plans. Undulating water, mists, and blooms can all be seen. Interlocking lines, circles, stars, squares, and triangles can also be found in mind-blowing mathematical schemes. Rehashing plans is a common occurrence in projects.

Most patterns, in general, have a meaning or purpose. For example, the precious stone shape (Hishi) is frequently seen in Japanese interior design. The bee colony (Kikko) plan is regarded as a symbol of good fortune.

5. Move Paper or Fusible Interfacing

With Sashiko you follow the pattern onto your texture utilizing white exchange paper or fusible interfacing

Sashiko Thimble is a discretionary item.

When working with lengthy Sashiko needles to fasten vast mathematical lines in your work, this is quite useful. With the metal plate in your palm, you use this thimble like a ring. You may press your needle through the texture with this thimble.

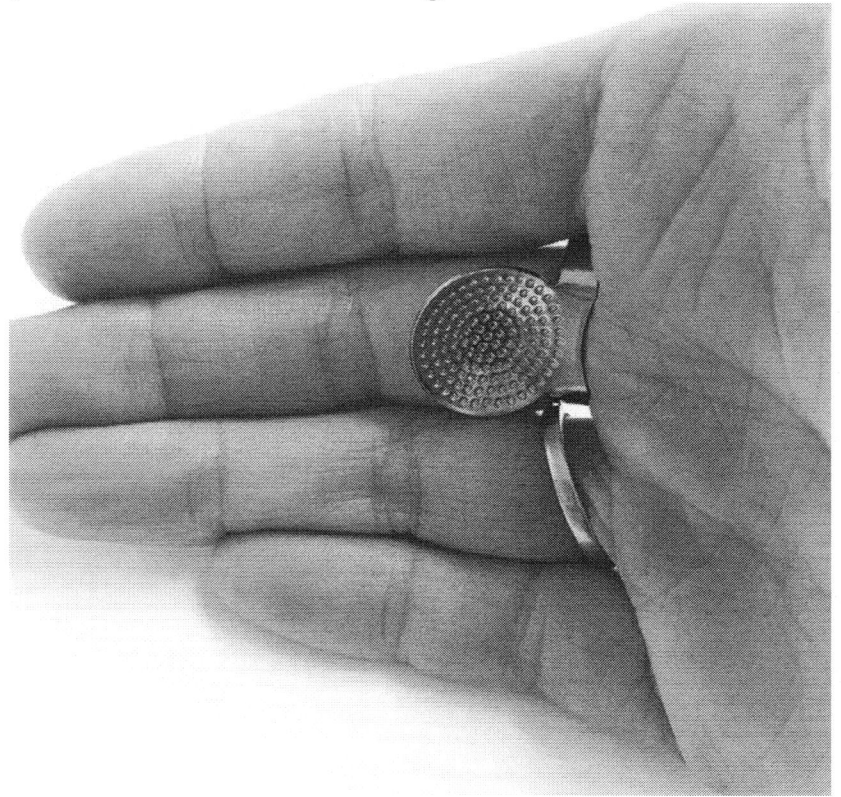

7. Optional: Hoop or Frame for Embroidery

It helps to use a weaving loop to make straight and equal lines.

8. Weaving Scissors

You'll utilize the weaving scissors to cut of every one of your strings.

9. Discretionary: Ruler

When chipping away at a pattern with long straight lines it is helpfull to utilize a ruler to follow your pattern.

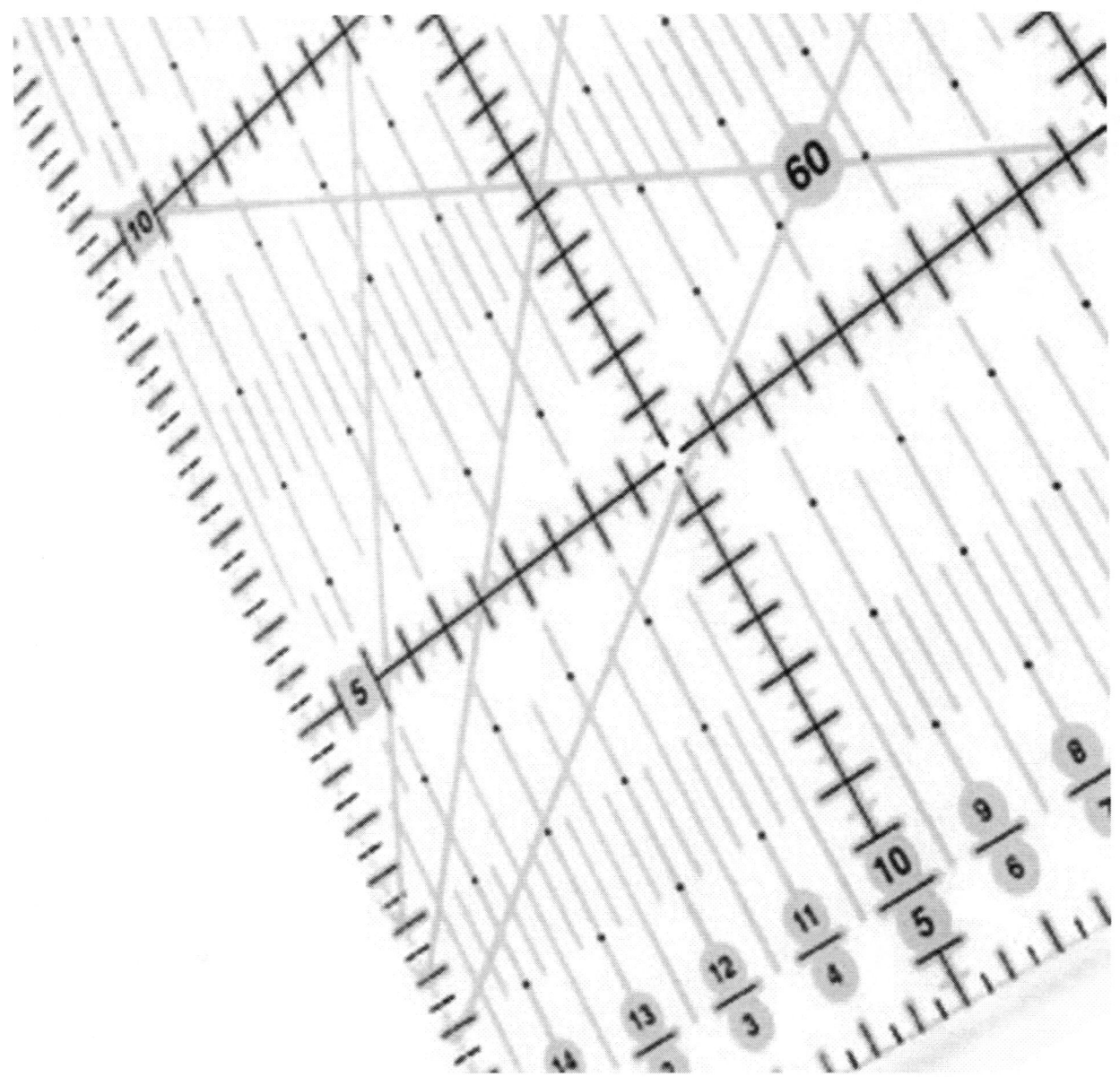

CHAPTER TWO

HOW TO FOLLOW A SASHIKO PATTERN

The means beneath clarify how you can move a Sashiko pattern to your texture. We utilize white exchange paper as we are sewing on dull blue texture.

It is consistently a decent practice to wash your texture prior to moving the pattern and beginning to join, as it might somehow contract in future.

Stage 1

Lay your texture level on the table. Iron if necessary. Lay a sheet of white exchange paper on top of it. I   include the pattern and use it as your top layer.

Stage 2

Utilize a pencil to follow the pattern. Push adequately hard and you will see white markings on your texture. In the event that this is your first time – check the strategy on a test piece. Guarantee you don't move the pattern while following it.

Stage 3

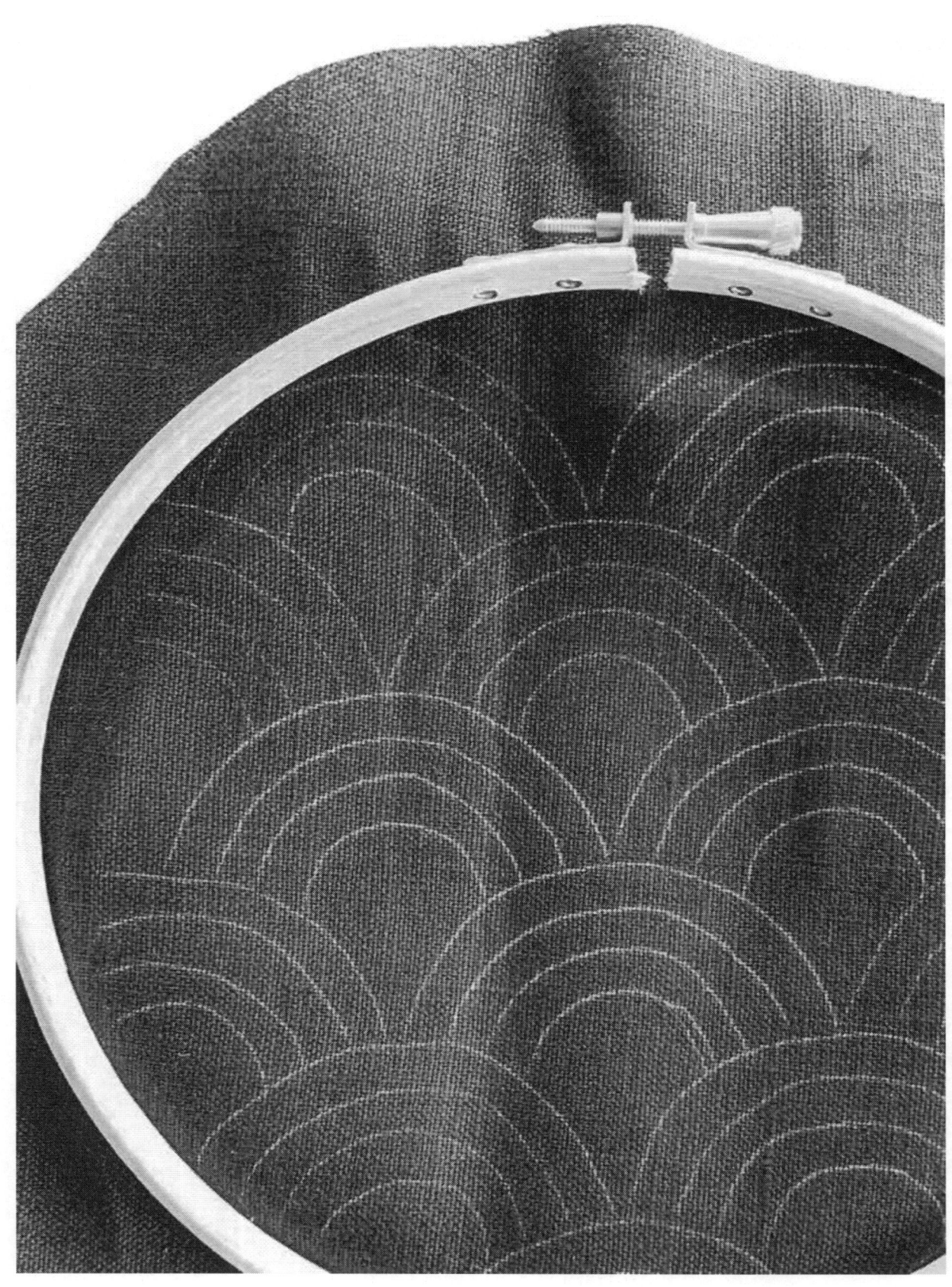

Eliminate the pattern and following paper and you will see the white markings on your texture. Prepared for your sashiko join! Also, no concerns on the off chance that you committed a couple of errors. You can undoubtedly clean them out after you get done with sewing.

Tip: if your pattern is greater than your following paper you can cautiously move the following paper under your pattern as you follow the lines. Take care not to move the pattern

How to follow a Sashiko pattern to your texture utilizing fusible interfacing?

For greater undertakings you may get a kick out of the chance to utilize interfacing to move a pattern to your texture. The means beneath clarify how you can do this

Stage 1

Measure your Sashiko and create your pattern on the table and spot out a piece of white thread interfacing it over it. Guarantee you have the paste side (the glossy unpleasant side) down. Tape the sides of the interfacing on the table.

Star Tip: Use a piece of interfacing bigger than your sashiko project.

Stage 2

Follow the pattern with a fine tip perpetual texture marker onto your interfacing. When following long straight lines it is useful to utilize a ruler

Stage 3

Take your interfacing and position it on the posterior of your texture with the paste side confronting your texture. Circuit it set up with your iron. Start in the focal point of your plan. Lift your iron and set as opposed to sliding your iron to dodge deforming your plan.

Keep in mind: the side with the interfacing is the rear of your task.

CHAPTER THREE

THE MOST EFFECTIVE METHOD TO SASHIKO JOIN BIT BY BIT DIRECTIONS

Subsequent to moving your texture you are prepared to begin Sashiko Stitching! Better believe it! Beneath you will discover bit by bit guidelines to kick you off.

A couple of fundamental rules you can follow during your sewing:

- With Sashiko sewing you fundamentally make a running line.

- Sashiko join are in every case longer on the highest point of the texture than they are on the posterior.

- Stitch as equitably as possible. Whatever length you make your top join, make all your top lines that length, and whatever length you make your rear fastens, make all your posterior lines that length. A general guideline for the length of your fastens is to make posterior sewed 1/3 the length of the top join. Join around 2-3 fastens per cm (~4 to 8 for each inch).

- Ensure your top join don't cross each other at an intersection of lines.

Stage 1

Cut around 60 – 75 cm (24 – 30 inch) of string, and get it through the eye of your needle. We utilized every one of the 6 strands of the 6 abandoned weaving floss.

When dealing with a mathematical plan, pick a long vertical or even line to start your sewing.

When chipping away at a pattern with round shapes pick the longest queue you can discover.

Stage 2

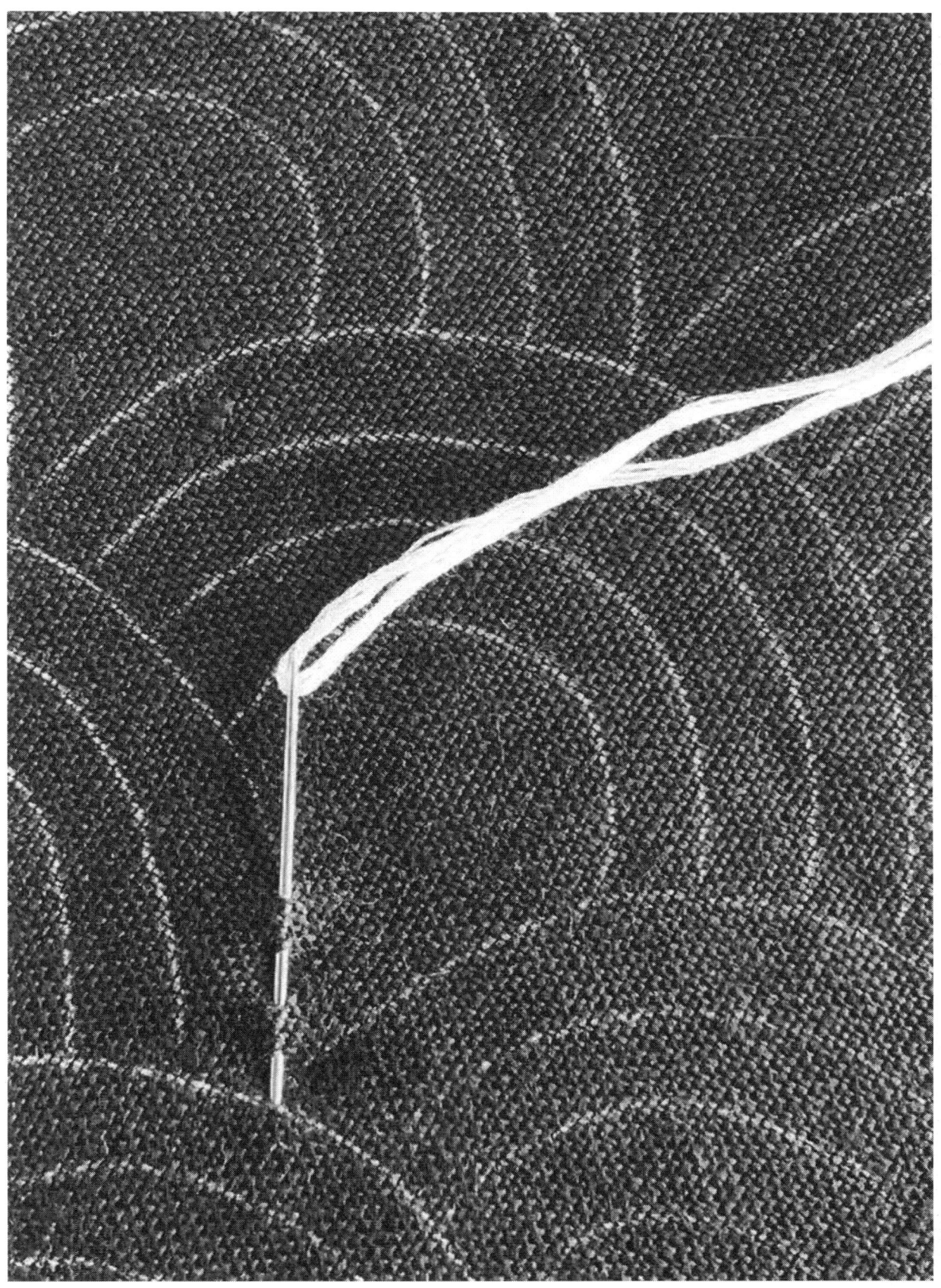

Supplement your needle 5 cm (2 inch) along the beginning line and take a few lines back towards the start.

Stage 3

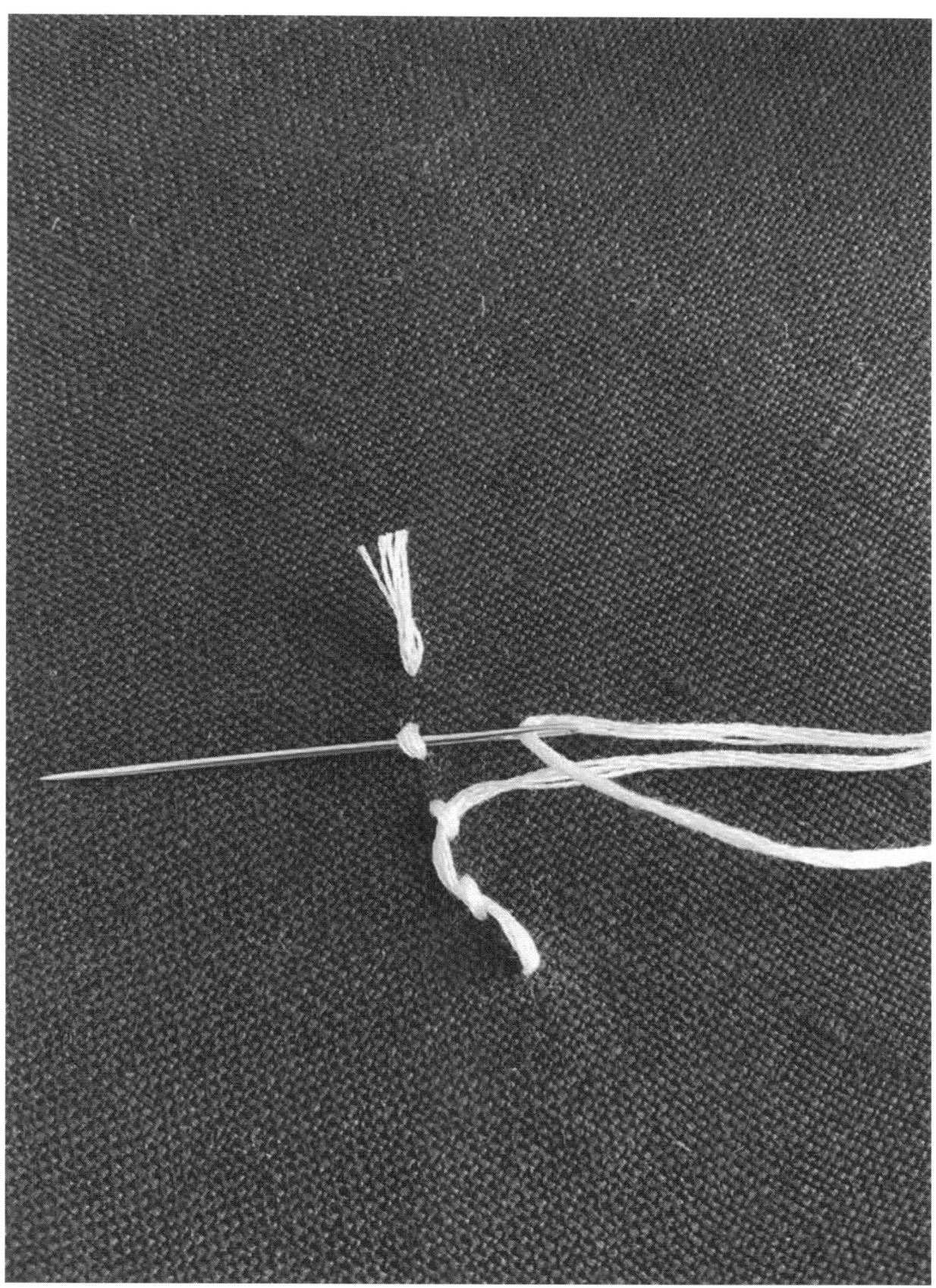

Carry your needle to the rear of your texture. Secure the principal string by passing your needle back through the lines on the rear of the texture.

Stage 4

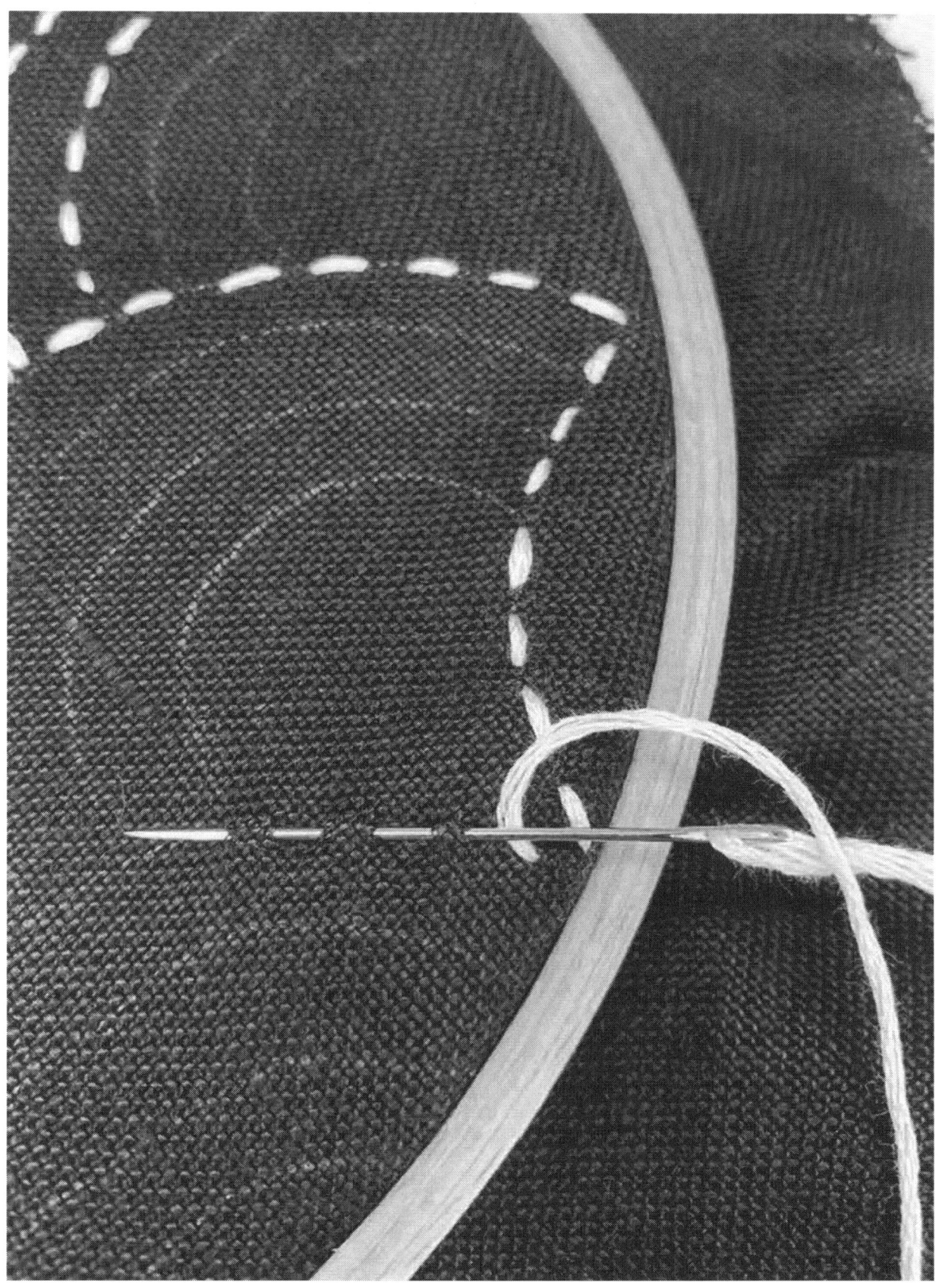

Carry your needle to the front side of the texture and proceed with join along the line. Put however many join on your needle as you find agreeable, at that point delicately get the needle through your texture.

Stage 5

Rehash making fastens. Your last line of a line should come up precisely at the corner. At the point when required, change the line lenght of the last scarcely any cm's (inch) to get it going.

Start your first line the following way very near the corner fasten.

When turning bearing, don't pull your string excessively close. It's better in the event that you

leave a touch of slack on the posterior (as imagined).

Stage 6

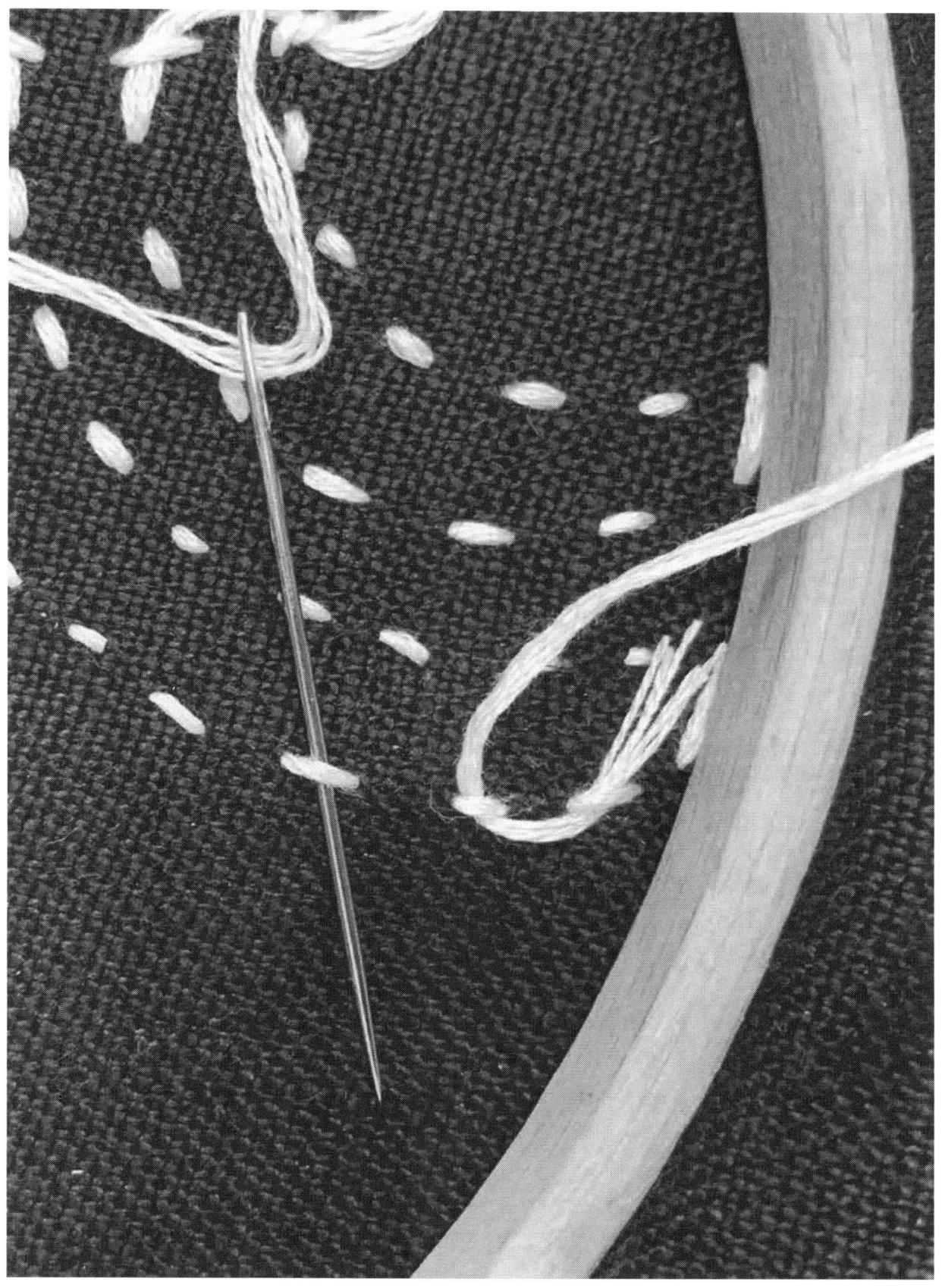

At the point when you are going to complete a string, carry your needle to the rear. Pass the needle through a couple of lines in crisscross modus and remove any abundance yarn.

Secure new strings by going them through a couple of prior made lines on the rear.

Sashiko grouping in sewing

Work lines individually. Start in one corner and work towards the opposite side of the texture. Backpedal on another line towards the first side.

Most patterns accompany markings to control you how to fasten them. The photos beneath show the sewing direction of two well known plans.

Sashiko Stitch Like a Pro Tips

Be cautious where lines cross. Work as exact as possible. You get the best outcome when you attempt to make the primary join toward every path to start at a similar separation from the focal point of the intersection. This implies that on the rear of your texture you may have to make a more extended line to arrive at a similar beginning stage at the following line.

Get your needle delicately through the texture! Try not to pull your needle excessively hard, as this may make your texture pucker. It's simpler to fix join which are excessively free than those that are excessively close. Free join can be modified by tenderly pulling your string on the posterior of the texture.

When chipping away at long queues, utilize a Sashiko thimble! You utilize this thimble like a ring with the metal plate within your palm. Utilizing this thimble you can push your needle through the texture.

Unwind. Take a taste from your number one beverage and go slowly ;-).

The most effective method to complete your Sashiko project

At the point when you've finished sewing your pattern there's a couple of steps left and you're done!

Stage 1

Eliminate any exchange lines made with the carbon paper. You can do this via cautiously handwashing your work. Or then again by utilizing a water shower.

Stage 2

Iron your work from the posterior. Start in your texture. Pull your iron here and there as you move along the texture, as opposed to sliding it over the texture.

Stage 3

Edge your first Sashiko in a weaving circle. Or on the other hand transform your Sashiko project into a pad cover, decorative spread, napkin, or toiletry pack. You can likewise make shocking articles of clothing with your undertaking.

49 by 50 cm Premium Blue Ecological Sashiko Fabric

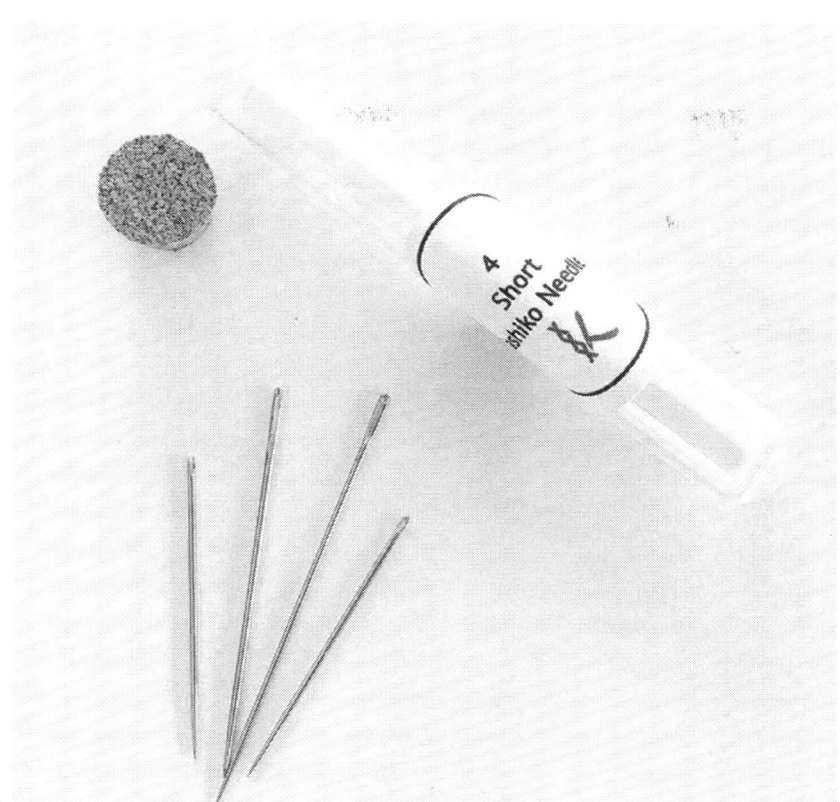

- Set of 4 short Sashiko Needles in a cylinder

-

2 sheets of white exchange paper | water erasable

-

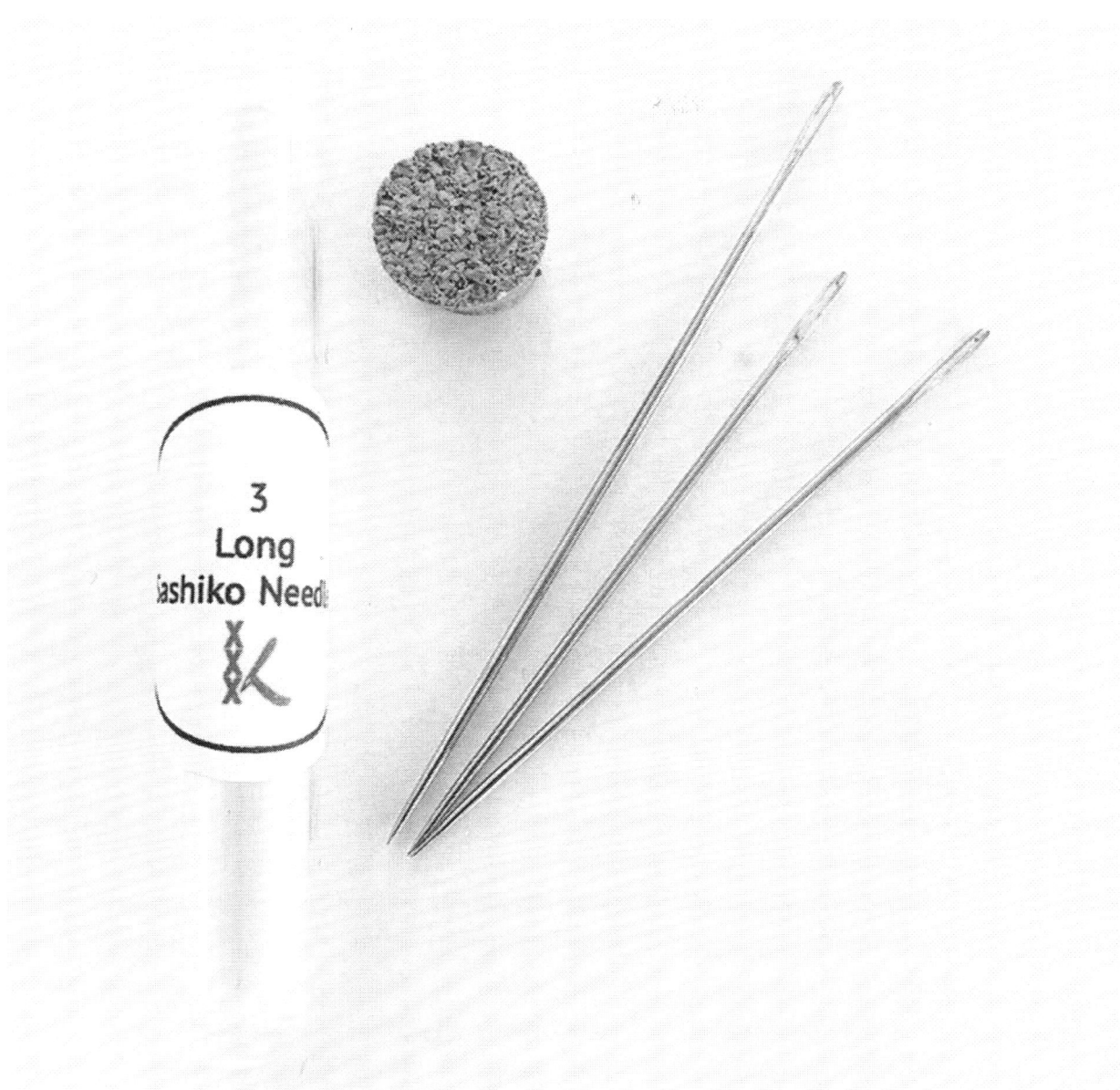

Set of 3 Long Sashiko Needles in a cylinder

-

 100 by 150 cm Premium Navy Blue Sashiko Ecological fabric (Linen)

-

Sashiko ring thimble with plate One size fits all

- 40 x 90 cm white iron on glue Vlieseline

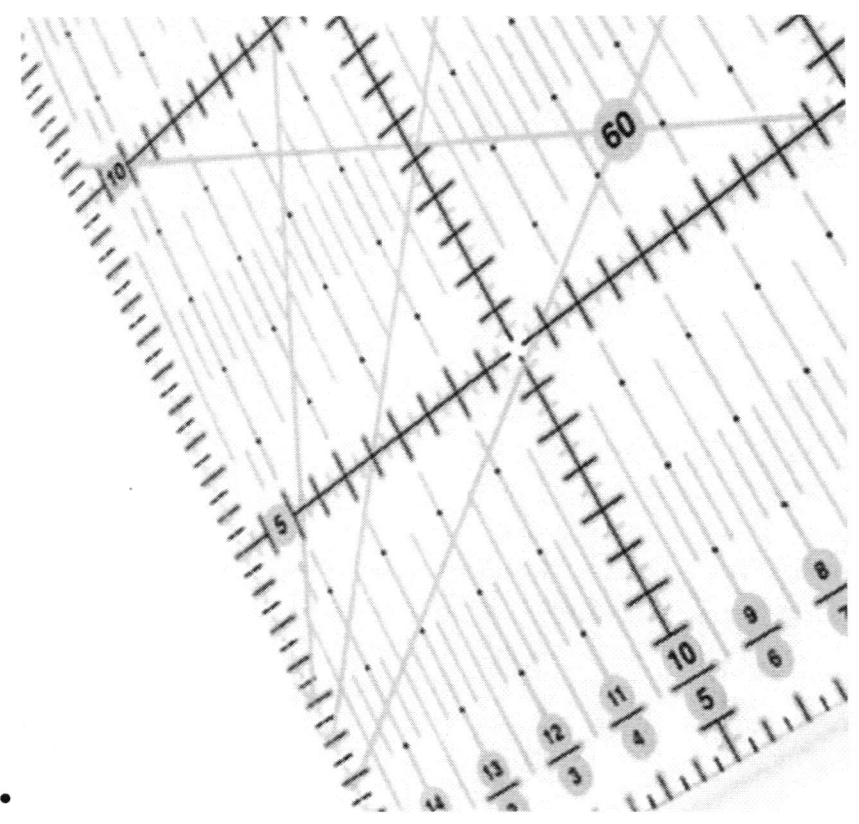

Prym omnigrid ruler 15 x 60 cm long blanket ruler

CHAPTER FOUR

THE MOST EFFECTIVE METHOD TO SASHIKO STITCH, BEGINNING WITHOUT A KNOT, DECIDING STITCH LENGTH AND MAKING GOOD CORNERS

In a new instructional exercise we covered my number one technique for how to get your sashiko plan onto your texture. This is section two of that four section sashiko instructional exercise. This time we will cover

- how to begin your sewing without tying your string,
- how to deal with your line length,
- and how to choose what the line length ought to be,
- also, how to hold your texture, load fastens on the needle, and turn a sharp corner.

Prepared to proceed?

You ought to have your sashiko configuration combined to the rear of your texture and prepared to join.

Ideally you have viewed how to utilize sashiko string without it turning into a tangled wreck and you are prepared to string your sashiko needle with a length of sashiko string.

Stage 1.

String your sashiko needle. Pick one corner of the external square shape to start your sewing. About an inch or so along the line, and away from the corner, embed your needle and take a few lines back toward the corner. You will feel like you are moving in reverse since you are! It is significant that your needle come up directly in the corner on the last join.

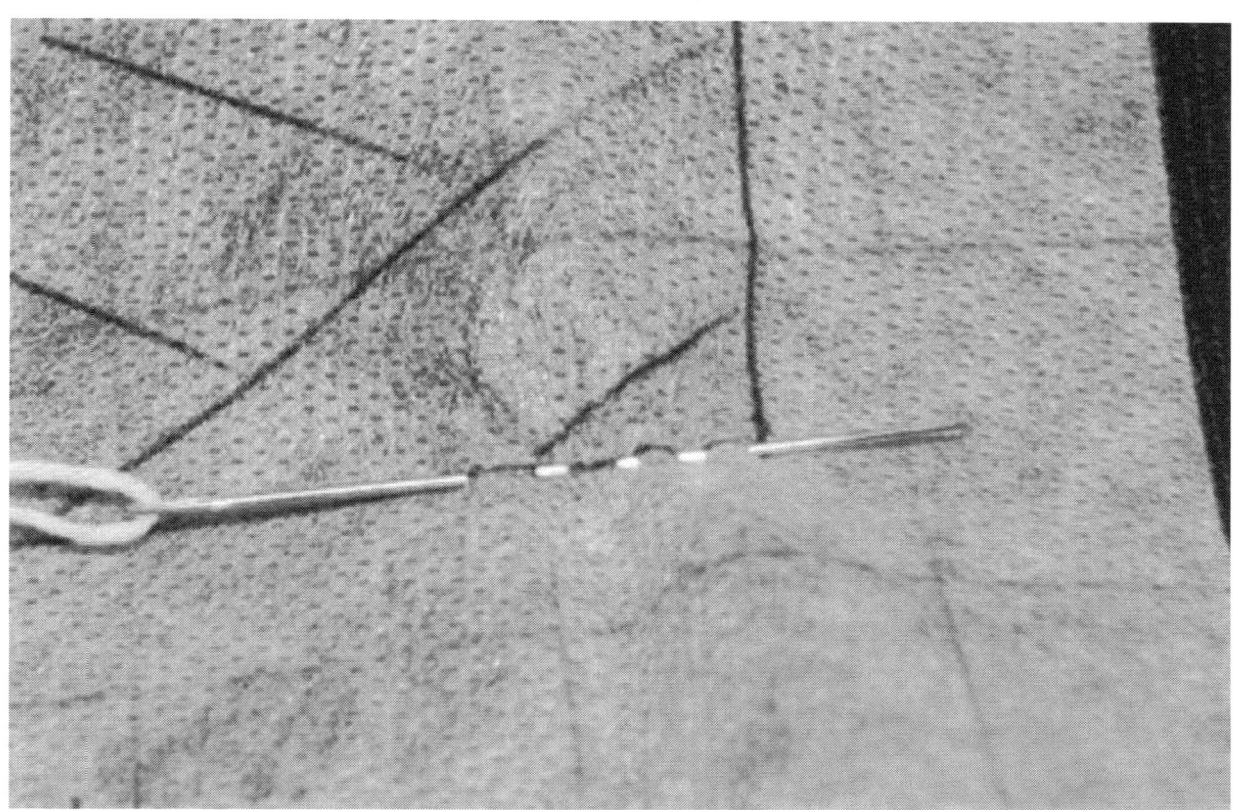

There are three things to remember here.

1. You are sewing from the back with this exchange strategy. Attempt it. A few strings, you will think that its agreeable. (I referenced previously, however a to the side once more, those yellow lattice lines on my interfacing in the photographs have nothing to do with our instructional exercise. They incidentally turned out to be on the interfacing I utilized)

2. Sashiko fastens are in every case longer on top (the completed side) of the texture than they are on the underside, and it is essential to keep your lines a similar length. This is to say, whatever length you make your line on the top, make every one of your fastens on the top that length, and make all you lines on the underside 1/3 that length.

3. How long should the line really be on the top (the completed side of the texture)? About the length of a grain of rice! For this weight cotton I am utilizing 4 or 5 fastens (on the completed right side) per inch. You should discover the length that feels good to you. Sashiko sewing resembles penmanship, unmistakable to the person.

Stage 2

Bring your needle back through the fastens on the rear of the texture to get it.

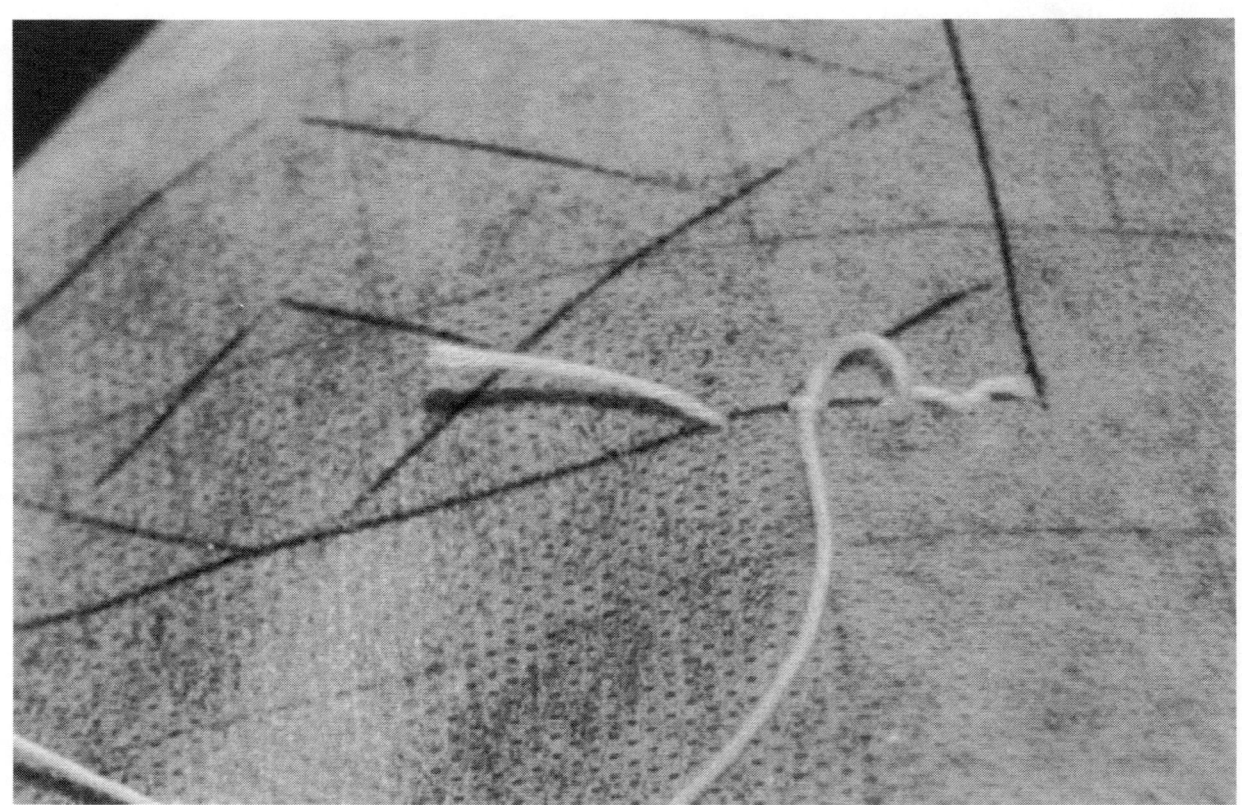

Start ensuing strings by passing them under a couple of fastens on the rear of your texture, and end them similarly. The principal string is the just a single you need to do the line in reverse strategy.

Stage 3

Take a few additional join along the sashiko sewing line, gathering them up on your needle. In the event that this is off-kilter from the start, gather a couple before you get them through. With training it will get simpler. The significant thing to consider at this stage is keeping your join length and spaces even. Here is a tip: watch the finish of your needle when it gets through the texture, and pull it back until you see a similar measure of it's tip each time.

It takes some training to get your lines to stream along equitably dispersed, however not a ton of training, so attempt to unwind and approve of 'sufficient' until further notice. On the off chance that you get to the furthest limit of the string and disdain what you have done, its simple to haul it out and do once more! It's smarter to push ahead than to attempt to consummate this initial not many fastens.

When putting the lines on the needle I hold the needle in my correct hand very still, and feed the join on with my left hand. Continue on, its talent will come to you!

I additionally assemble the overabundance texture up in my avoided hand so it is held with regard to the route as I join. It doesn't make any difference the amount you wrinkle it, the plan will not wear off and the texture will simply get more pleasant. On the off chance that it gets to wrinkled to deal with inevitably, press it out and continue.

Stage 4

Get the needle through the texture and smooth the lines back by running your fingers back over them. A difficult you need to try not to is have the texture pucker, so every time you get your needle through it is a decent practice to watch that the texture and lines are extended level and the string isn't tight.

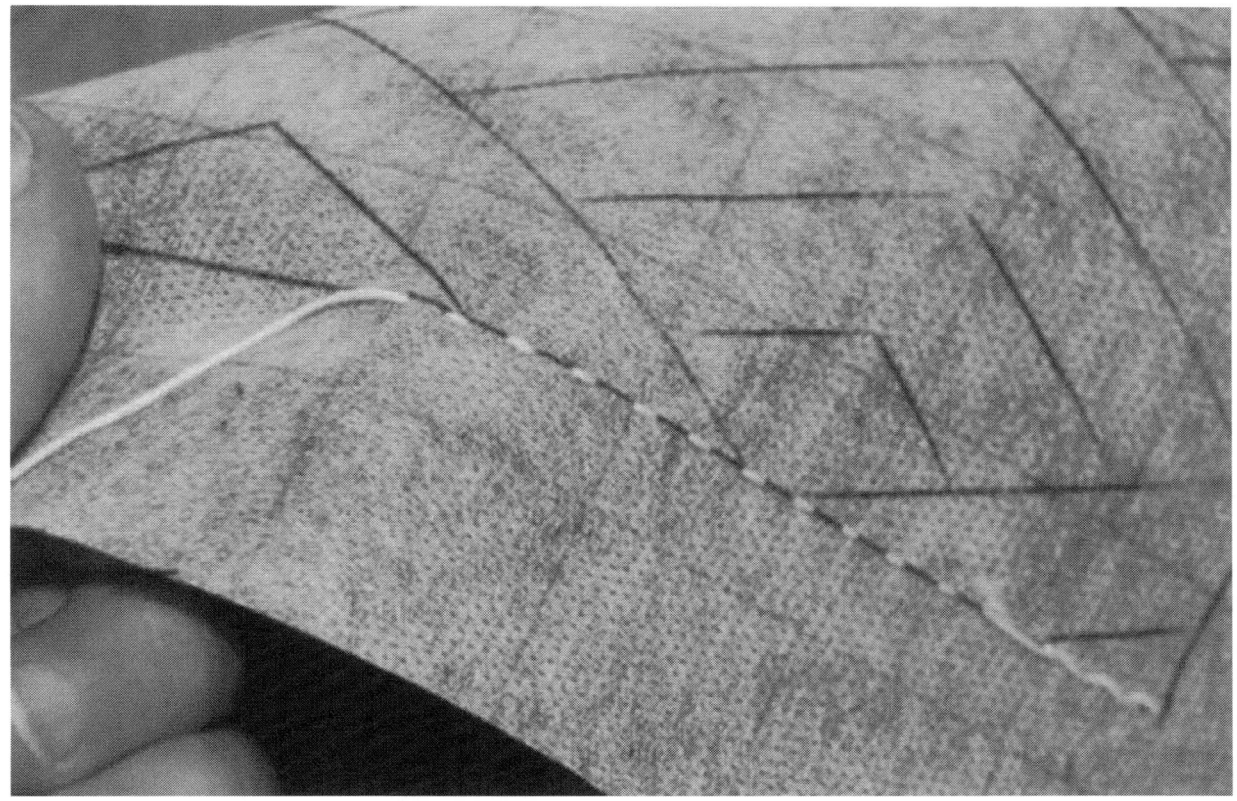

Keep on sewing along this first line until you arrive at the corner. Your last fasten should end precisely on the corner. On the off chance that that doesn't occur you should change your join lengths a little on the last couple of creeps to get it going.

A smidgen of variety in the length of your fastens won't hurt your undertaking, rather it is the thing that gives that quality we esteem such a huge amount close by sewn materials.

Stage 5

Turning a corner. At the point when you have arrived at the corner and your keep going join is actually on that corner, you need to take your next fasten close yet not contacting that corner line.

Also, this is significant, you need to be certain you leave a touch of slack in the string on the back at corners (like a little circle). This circle should in any case be there after you have pulled every one of the fastens smooth and level. Sashiko string is 100% cotton and it will recoil a little when washed. This is as it ought to be, and will give you a lovely piece of surface, yet on the off chance that you don't leave slack on the rear of your sewing, over the long haul it will turn out to be excessively close and ruin your plan. The denser the sashiko sewing on your venture, the more significant this becomes.

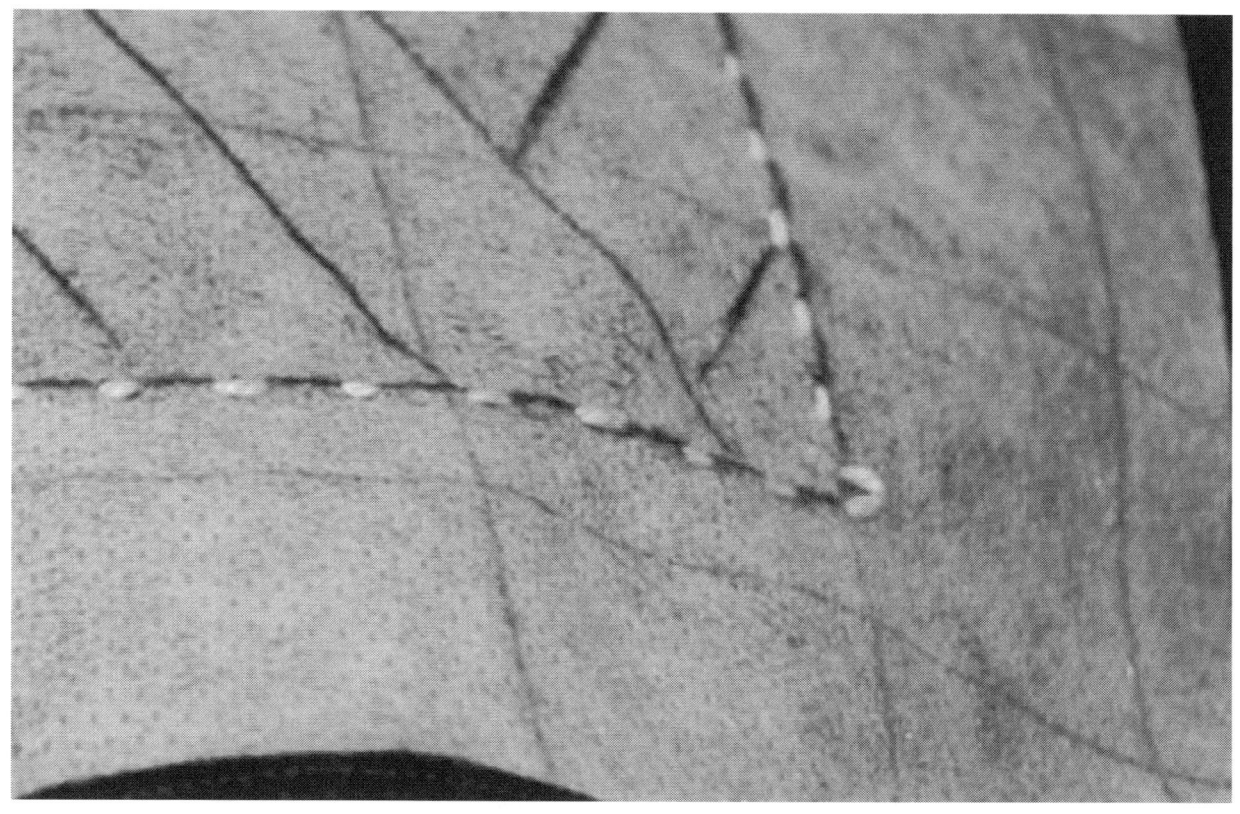

HOW TO DO SASHIKO EMBROIDERY

A type of beautiful support, or utilitarian weaving, Sashiko sewing started in Japan out of reasonable need during the Edo time (1615-1868). Initially it was utilized to fasten together layers of texture for additional strength and warmth, and furthermore for patching worn pieces of clothing. It's made from running line, which is one of the most straightforward weaving lines to utilize and learn. Current

Sashiko takes motivation from conventional plans and uses them for more embellishing purposes on sacks, articles of clothing, stitching boards and numerous other imaginative undertakings.

Utilizing a clean differentiating string, Sashiko is easily exquisite, and it's a smart (and brisk) approach to add an individual touch to shop-brought articles of clothing and blessings. Gracious, and did we notice, it's truly simple to will grasps with as well? Attempt our two plant pots which are the ideal Sashiko projects for amateurs and afterward take a stab at adjusting the method to use with shapes with our free Sahsiko pattern PDF to add cloud themes to textures. These three things are official Sashiko projects for fledglings to help you capitalize on this simple method.

Stage 1

There are various methods of moving plans onto texture and for this task we have utilized a framework base that can be stamped straightforwardly onto the texture. Measure and cut your texture and afterward press level. Lay the texture on a table, getting with concealing tape. Utilizing a stamping pen and a reasonable ruler, make a 5mm matrix. Pick a shade of pen that will appear on your texture.

Stage 2

Tie a bunch in your string and work Running Stitch over and under the texture following the pattern on the texture leaving a hole where the matrix lines meet. Try not to pull the fastens too firmly and attempt to continue to work in columns. Utilize an expert Sashiko needle on the off chance that you can, as these will in general be longer than normal weaving needles, which empowers you to work more lines all at once.

Stage 3

At the point when you arrive at the finish of a column, leave a more extended fasten/circle freely on the rear of the texture to ease starting with one line then onto the next. This is truly critical to guarantee the strain of the sewing is even. At the point when you reach the finish of the string, make a bunch over the string on the back to get. Start another string with a bunch, ensuring it is safely affixed on the back.

Stage 4

Develop a plan by sewing in straight lines in various headings. Where the lattice lines meet, space the join so they don't contact one another. This makes a lot neater and smoother finish to the sewing. The holes between the join can be tiny as demonstrated here or bigger spaces can be left in the event that you like. Trial until you are content with the plan.

Plant pot Sashiko patterns and tasks for amateurs

You will require

- Cotton texture: (enormous pot: 40x110cm, naval force), (little pot: 40x60cm, yellow)

- Medium weight iron-on interfacing:(large pot: 40x60cm), (little pot: 30x35cm)

- White texture pencil or dark warmth erasable pen

- Clear quilter's ruler

- Sashiko string: white

- Sashiko needles

- Basic weaving pack

Stage 1

Cut the texture as follows:

Enormous pot: two pieces 21x50cm, for the body external and coating; two 17cm breadth circles for the base external and covering.

Little pot: two pieces 17x30cm, for the body external and coating; two 11cm measurement circles for the base external and covering.

Take the body external and imprint a 5mm framework situated 2cm from the short side edges and 2.5cm from the base long edge. Utilize a white texture pencil on dim textures or a dark warmth erasable pen on light textures The lattice should be 18 squares high for the huge pot and 15 squares high for the little pot.

Stage 2

Utilizing white Sashiko string and a Sashiko needle, fasten the plan utilizing Running Stitch. The little pot is sewed by working sets of vertical lines down the texture.

Stage 3

Then, work vertical lines between the sets, at that point work flat lines across. Work each line in turn, turning toward the finish of each line. Recall not to cross the fastens but rather to leave a hole between them.

Stage 4

To work the enormous pot, fasten the principal line following stage 02 on the How to do Sashiko weaving segment. Work each line in turn, turning toward the end. Work the following line even to the main recollecting not to cross the stitches. Finally, work askew lines across the texture – first from base left to upper right, at that point from base option to upper left.

Stage 5

When the Sashiko sewing is done, sliced interfacing to a similar size as the external body and base. Trim the 1cm crease stipend off in general, at that point press to the WS of each. Sew the short edges of texture RS together. Make quarter blemishes on the circle and on the base edge of the external body. Pin the external body and external base RS confronting, coordinating with the stamped focuses. Line together in general, cut the crease remittance and press the creases open.

Gather the coating similarly utilizing the covering body and coating base, yet this time leave a 3cm turning hole in the focal point of the body side crease.

Stage 6

Spot the covering inside the external so they are RS confronting and coordinating with top crude edges and side creases. Pin and line together. Turn RS out through the hole in the short crease, at that point slip line to close the hole.

Push the covering inside the external and press. Topstitch around the top edge to neaten and hold the coating set up. Give the top edge to make a sleeve, at that point gladly show your number one plant in the Sashiko pot.

Stage 1

Stage 2

Then, position the followed plan on your texture and tack it set up. Keep the join little and flawless as this will assist with forestalling the tissue paper from moving. For bigger plans, you'll see it accommodating to tack across the center of the paper too. Trim any overabundance tissue paper as important.

Stage 3

Sashiko needles and strings are accessible yet we utilized white abandoned cotton and a sharp crewel needle. Beginning at the base of the plan, follow the framework by weaving the needle all through the texture along the pencil lines, taking consideration not to pucker the texture.

Stage 4

Keep working across the plan in a coherent request. When becoming corners, don't get the string through totally – leave a circle on the back to forestall puckering. Finish strings by weaving them through the rear of your join. When complete, cautiously tear away the tissue paper – hold the join as you do this to forestall them being pulled by the tissue paper.

CHAPTER FIVE

WAYS TO TRANSFER A SASHIKO DESIGN ONTO FABRIC (5 OF 5 FEATHERWEIGHT INTERFACING METHOD)

The most effective method to move your sashiko plan onto your texture prepared for sewing utilizing fusible featherweight interfacing

The pre-imprinted on texture, prepared to fasten, sashiko plans are magnificent, however restrict you in plans and textures. For those of you who need to go further, this is the remainder of five blog sections of five strategies you can utilize get a sashiko plan onto a texture of your decision!

After close to fifteen years of sashiko sewing, this is as yet my liked strategy for preparing a plan onto texture to be sewed. I like it best for a few reasons I'll advise you as we go on here.

The following is the way to do it, however fast form goes this way: follow the plan onto the interfacing, combine it to the rear of your texture. Join away.

I know, you are figuring you can't line from the back, however, you can! sashiko sewing (means wound sewing) is only a running fasten, and that implies it is a similar join on the front and the rear of the texture. So it doesn't really matter which side you fasten from, simply make sure to make the lines on the completed side somewhat more than the lines as an afterthought you are seeing (make lines on some unacceptable side 1/3 of the lines on the correct side)

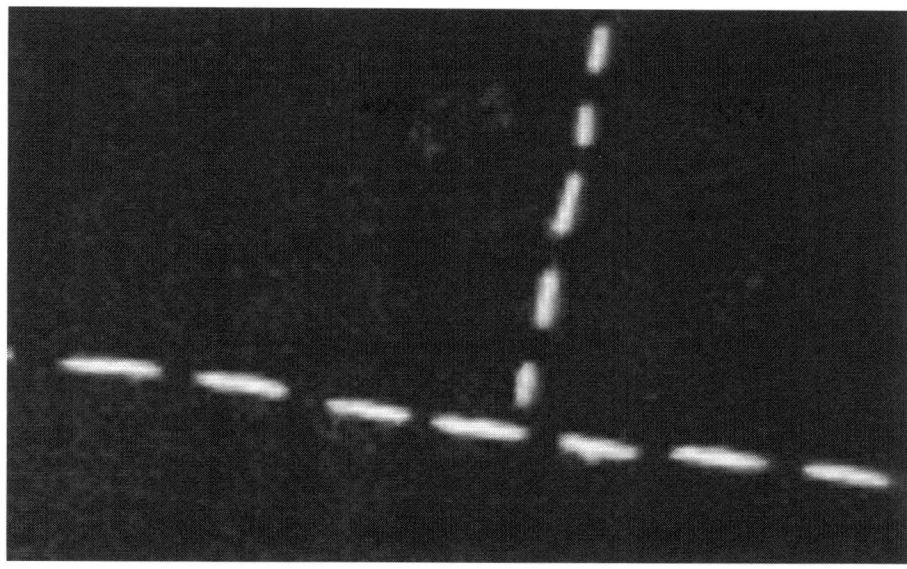

For what reason would you need to utilize this strategy?

1. Regardless of how much taking care of, or how large your sewing zone is, the lines will remain clear and dull. No disappearing.

2. It is simpler to make sure to leave sufficient minimal leeway pieces of string so the texture doesn't over fix as your sewing advances. You can likewise draw yourself a little circle where sewing lines get over one another to help keep them quite even on the completed side.

3. You can consolidate sashiko plans to make your own plans by following piece of one, at that point moving the interfacing to cover an alternate plan and following piece of it.

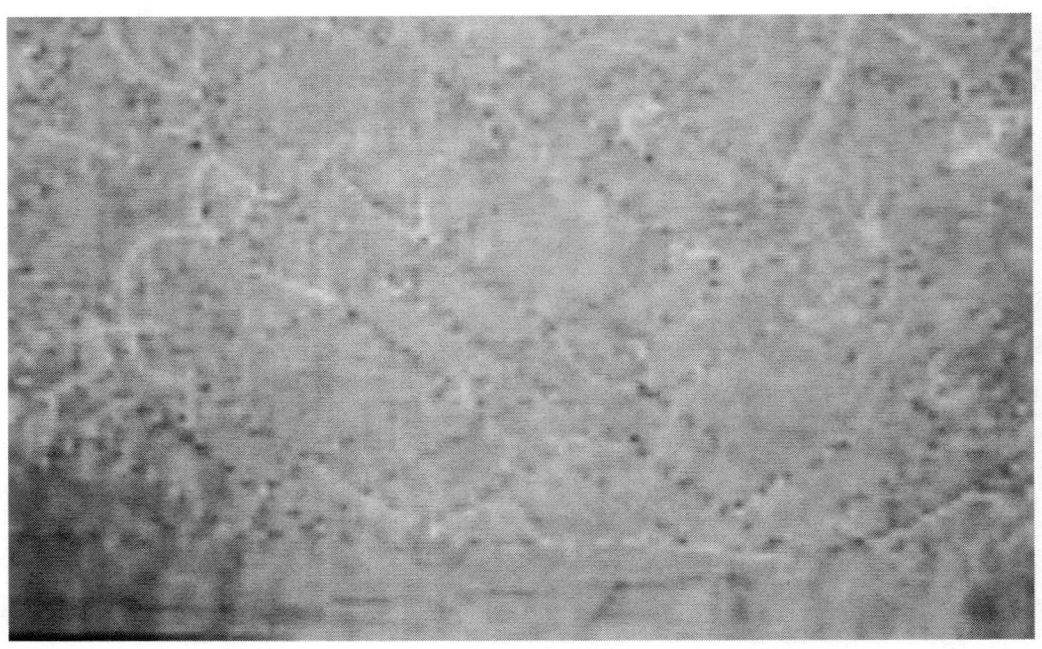

Here is the way to do it in detail:

Start with your sashiko plan, a perpetual ink fine tip pen, some white featherweight fusible interfacing (pellon) (non-woven is ideal), tape and a ruler.

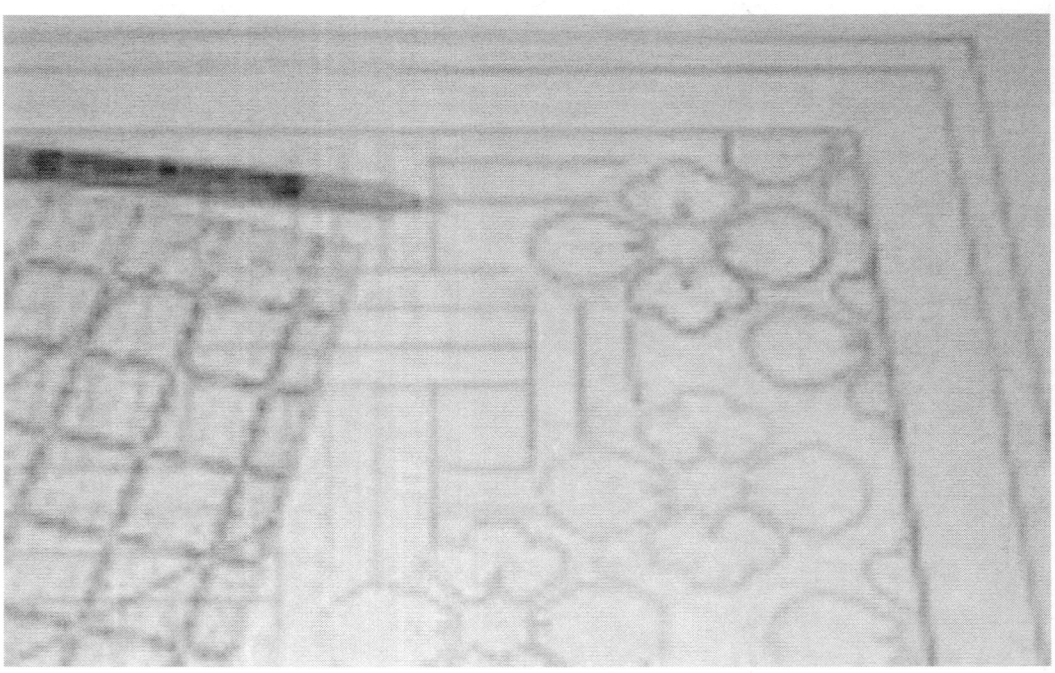

Tape the pattern to your table. Tape the interfacing paste side (the unpleasant side) down absurd. Tape it to the table. Utilizing the ruler and pen follow the plan onto the interfacing.

Presently lay the interfacing, stick side (harsh) down, over the rear of your texture and utilizing a medium warmth iron, meld the interfacing to the texture. (The paste dabs warmth, melts and wires the interfacing to the texture). Start in your plan and iron tenderly toward the edges. I lift and set my iron, as opposed to sliding it. This assists with holding the interfacing back from pulling rusty.

Presently your plan is safely on your texture. You will leave the interfacing on the texture when your sewing is done. There is no compelling reason to eliminate it as featherweight it is too light to even think about changing how the texture feels, and it will be canvassed in your completed venture.

Recollect you will join from the BACK of the texture. Attempt it before you conclude that you can't do it. It's in reality similarly as simple to line on the texture back, in addition to you have better control when you are becoming corners and getting over open spaces. Make sure to make your long fastens on the completed side tho!

SASHIKO

Texture, needle, and string:

Generally, Sashiko utilizes light hued string over hazier shades of texture. Once more, the most well known shade was dull blue or indigo, and white cotton string was utilized to work over it. Nowadays, you can generally explore different avenues regarding the shading shade of the texture or string to apply the Sashiko method.

The texture utilized famously was and still is cotton. Firmly woven even weave texture can be useful for Sashiko. Nowadays, silk and fleece is likewise getting up to speed with fame.

The Sashiko string is made of unadulterated cotton and has no sheen. It has a heavier look and is more bent than the Perle cotton string. On the off chance that chipping away at a cotton texture, the Sashiko string can be supplanted with Perle cotton (#5, ideally) or four strands of cotton floss. Obviously, various textures would have diverse string prerequisite. For example, while dealing with silk, you may utilize lighter or more slender strings.

Generally, the Sashiko needle is just about 2 inches in length with a little eye. This needle helps in taking numerous join at a time. It is ideal to dodge short needles as the sewing can get tedious and tedious. Attempt to utilize a long needle with a serenely open eye.

Sewing:

1. Keep the running join as even as could really be expected. Any lopsidedness will handily be appeared on the pattern.

2. The join on the front side of the texture is more than the one under. The overall proportion is 3:2.

3. Keeping the working string at a length of 20 crawls all at once. That will help in a happy with sewing.

The most effective method to start, proceed, and end:

Customarily, Sashiko doesn't permit to begin or end a join with a bunch. However, for its simplicity, we can utilize hitches where the opposite of the texture won't be utilized or appeared. For textures where converse will be appeared, utilize the conventional technique as following:

Consider that the fasten is worked from left to right.

Note that the covering of the couple of lines is the thing that gets the thread.Try keeping the closures of the string at teh invert side of the texture.

Cut the finishes of the string as close as conceivable to the texture to give a perfect appearance.

Beginning   Continuing with a stitch   Ending

Making turns:

1. At the point when the plans are reversible, you need to hold the back as slick as could be expected. Consequently, you need to remove the string every step of the way and conceal it under different strings. To accomplish this, follow a similar technique as you would to start or end a fasten generally. (Allude the representations above).

2. At the point when the opposite side of the texture is covered up, you can turn utilizing a similar string. You can convey the working

string at the rear of the material if the distance isn't in excess of an inch. Attempt to leave the conveying string free to try not to pucker of the texture.

Corners and Centers:

The corners ought to be kept sharp. for this, one of the join should fall on the corner. That is, the needle ought to one or the other come up or go in through the corner point. Some other impact other than what is appeared in the representation isn't right (See the various corners).

The focuses ought to be left open. It should look like as in this delineation. Anything separated from this isn't right.

Sewing orders:

Fundamentally, Sashiko follows the accompanying request of sewing. In any case, note that the sewing request relies upon the plan as well. A fasten is to be kept persistent quite far.

CHAPTER SIX

STEP BY STEP INSTRUCTIONS TO SASHIKO STITCH, ORDER OF STITCHING, CARRYING THREADS OR NOT, AND THINGS TO AVOID

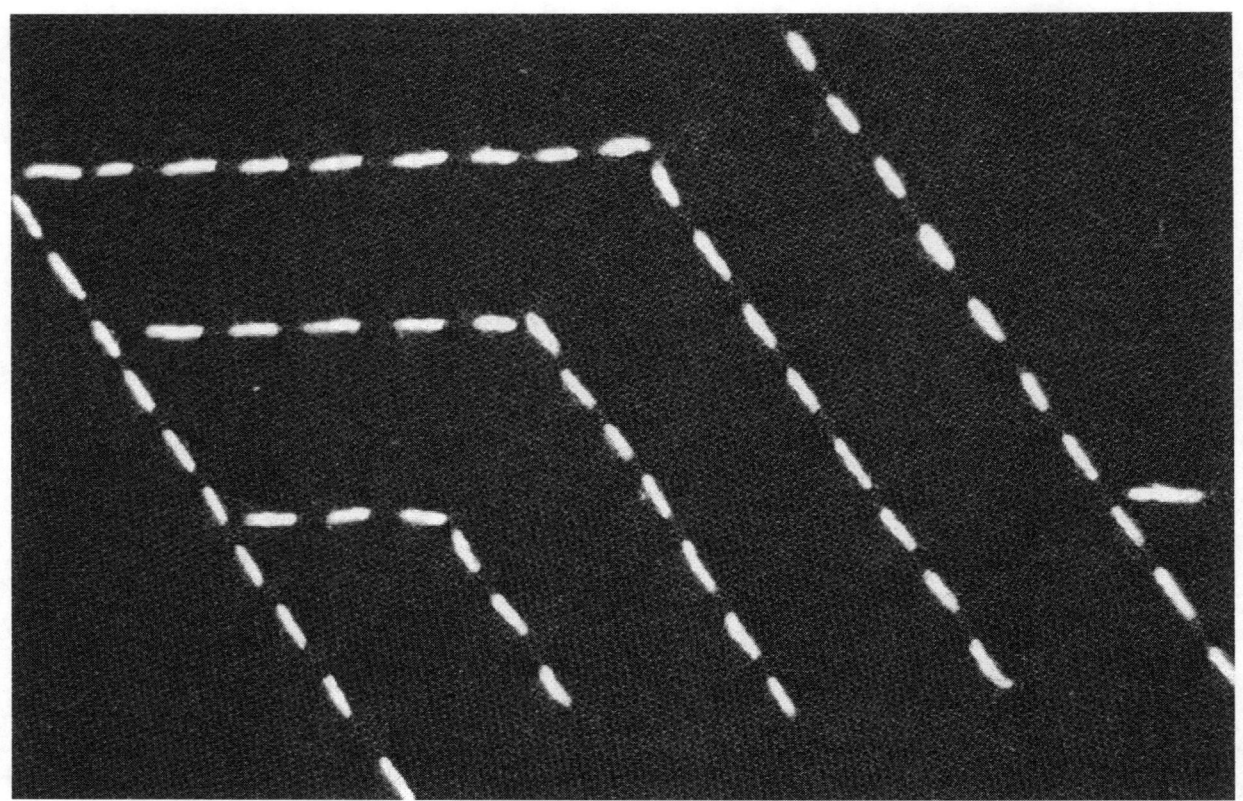

This is the third piece of our four section sashiko instructional exercise.

This time we take a gander at

where sashiko lines get through intersections or meet at points,

the 'request of sewing' in sashiko plans,

when to convey strings on the rear of your sashiko sewing,

and a few things you need to dodge in sashiko sewing.

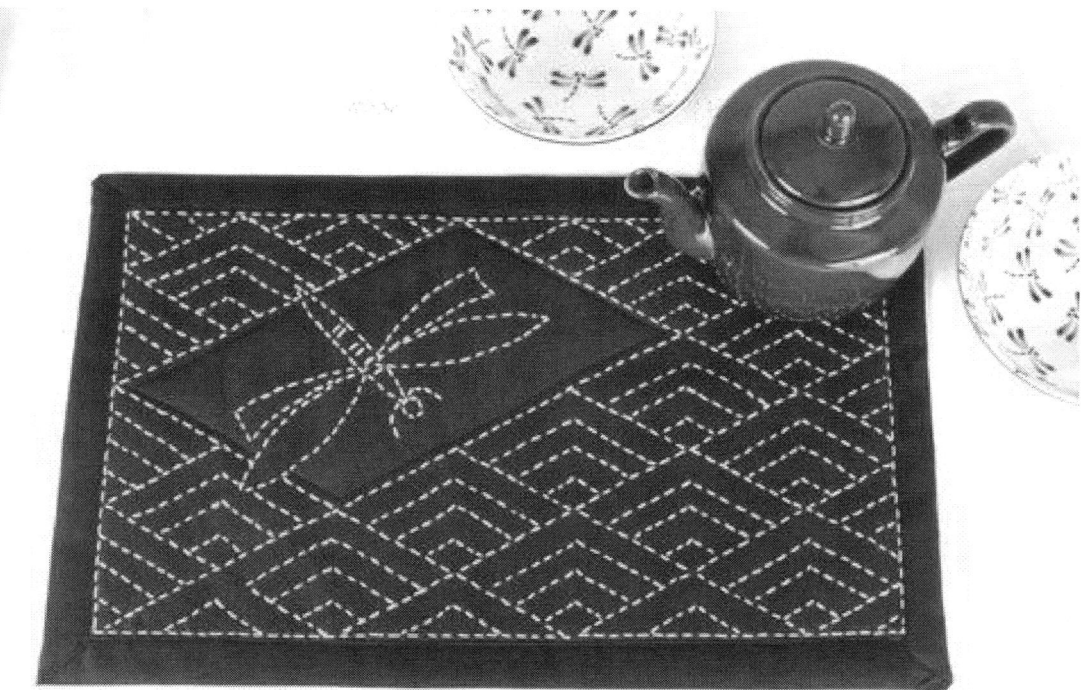

This is the sashiko plan we are utilizing for this instructional exercise. In parts one and two we moved the plan to the texture, figured out how to begin sewing without a bunch, settled on our line length, and figured out how to turn a decent corner. Furthermore, just to survey, we got a handle on the significance of leaving a little leeway in our strings on the rear of our task, isn't that so?

On the off chance that you didn't get done with sewing around the external line of the plan do that at this point.

Prepared to proceed?

Stage 1

The main thing we need to do now is to join throughout the entire the corner to corner lines from left to right, at that point all the excess long askew lines (these are the diagonals that go from one edge to another of the plan, we'll return to the more limited 'precious stone waves'). String your needle and start at the external edge. Secure your string by passing it under a couple of fastens in the external square shape close to where you mean to begin sewing. End your string in a similar way.

There is just a single new thing to consider while sewing these lines.

You need the tip of your needle to come up directly on the convergence of where a sewing line is crossed when you line the left to right diagonals. In this photograph I think my fasten is only the littlest piece excessively far, yet as I have said previously, sashiko sewing is exceptionally lenient and this smidgen of "not awesome" won't be seen in the general piece toward the end, so I am will leave it and proceed onward :-)

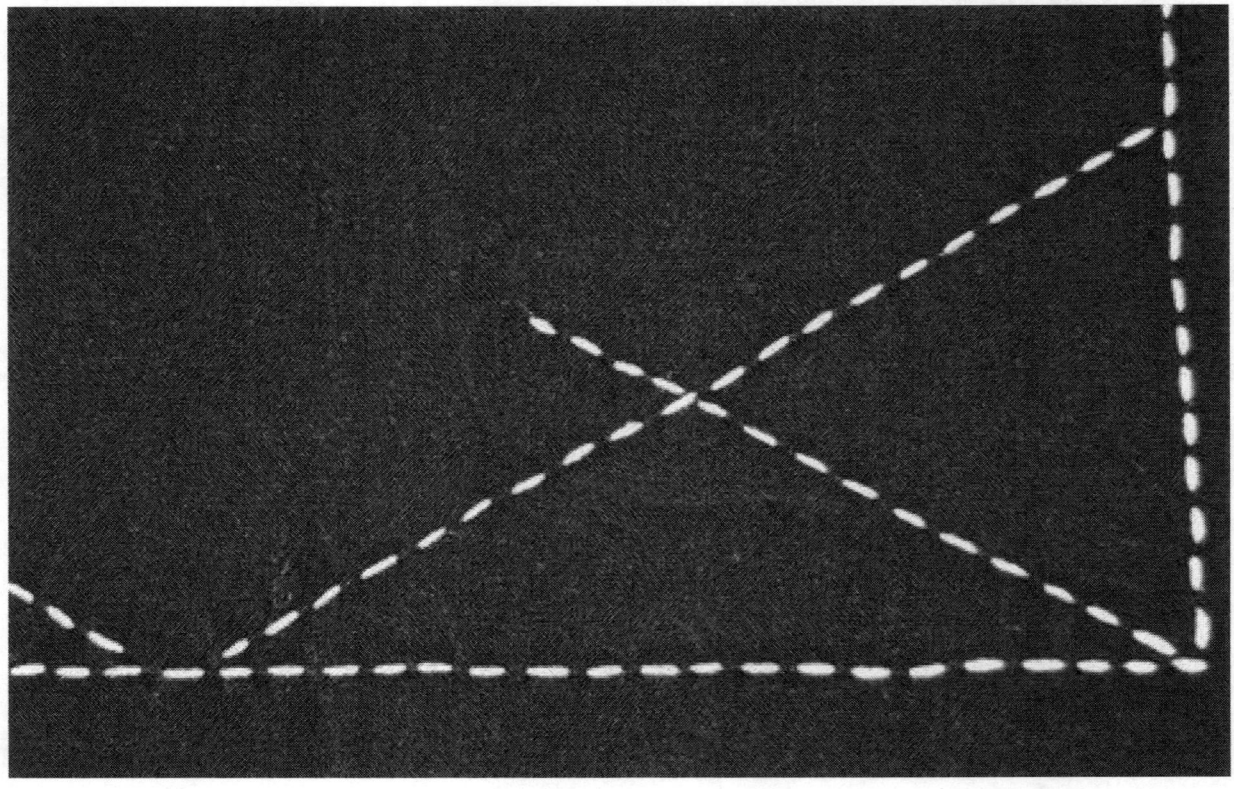

At the point when you line the intersection corner to corner lines you will space your lines over the convergence as demonstrated in the photo, being mindful so as not to get your needle in the fasten that finished in the convergence.

This will come effectively several crossing points as it is the thing that presence of mind makes you need to do in any case.

Stage 2

At the point when throughout the entire the lines have been sewed the time has come to join the jewel waves.

This is the place where we experience the 'request for sewing' now and again alluded to in sashiko sewing. Not being slanted to burn through valuable time or string, early sashiko stitchers utilized a request for sewing to get the most conceivable sewing out of each string. The idea is straightforward, rather than sewing singular shapes, line the long ceaseless lines, and when this is beyond the realm of imagination, plan your work so the spaces are just about as short as could be expected, and convey the string across the back.

Keep in mind: at whatever point you turn a corner or convey a string across a space on the back you need to leave a little leeway in your string. This is significant. In the event that you don't do it you will discover your texture starting to pucker as you get further along in your task.

Here are photographs to show you the sewing request for the precious stone wave plans:

start by weaving the finish of your string under a current few lines

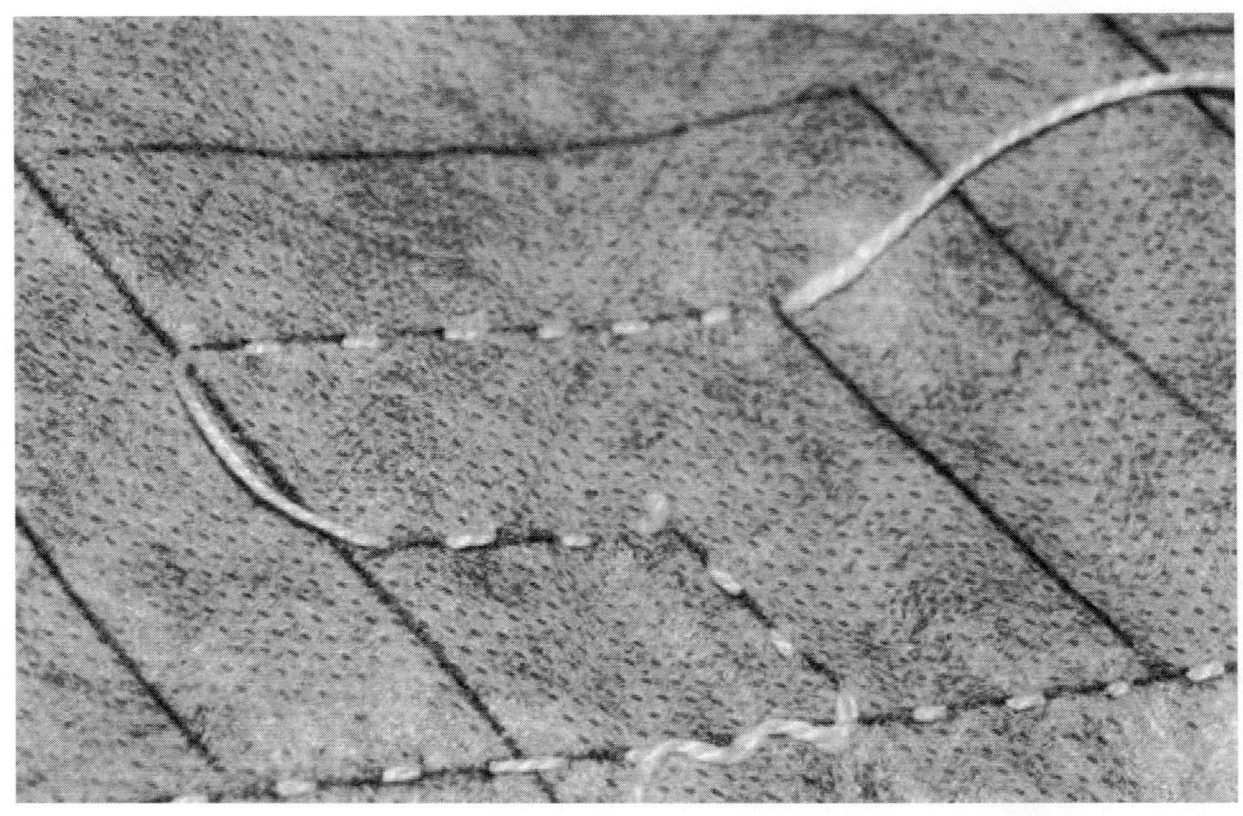

convey your string too the closest sewing line (leaving a little leeway)

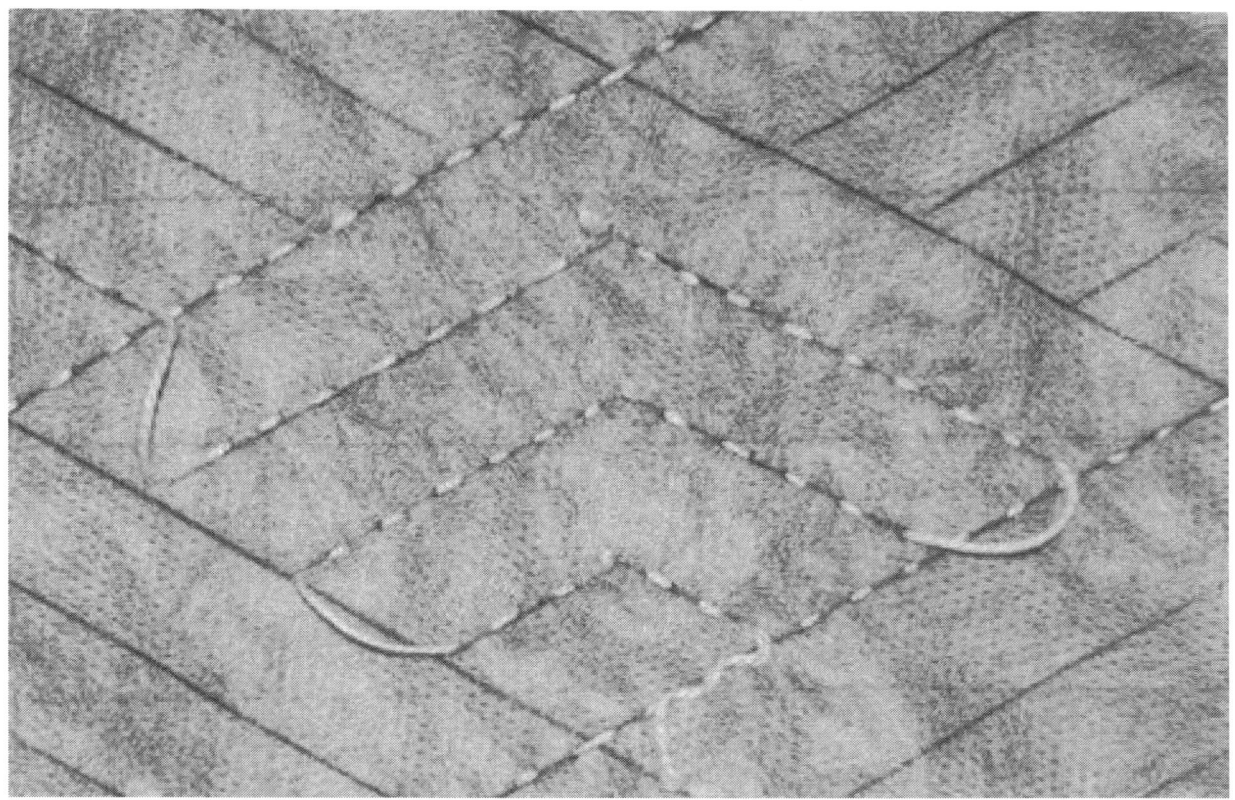

keep, going to the following closest arrangement of waves

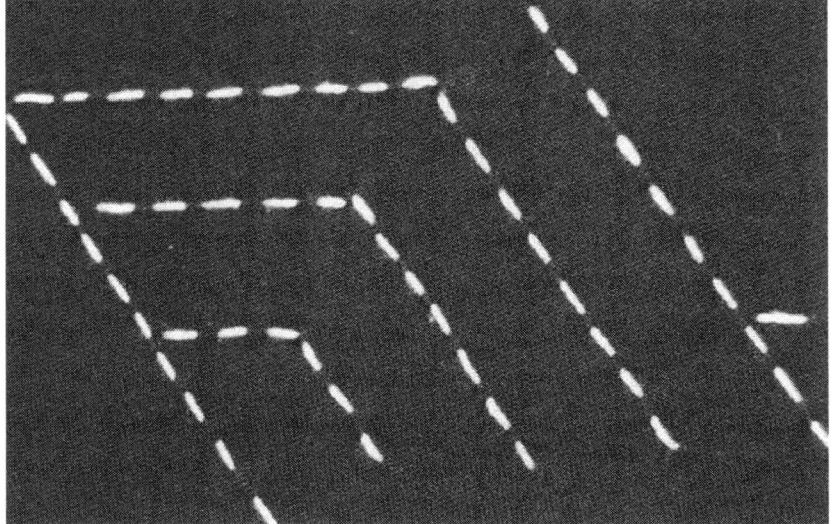

Here is a completed wave area and a few notes about the example photograph. The highest point of the center wave is the best done in this example, however when the piece is done the distinction in the others won't be recognizable.

Additionally notice in this photograph how the main line of the wave meets the long inclining line in such a y shape. This is somewhere else where you need your fasten to be somewhat nearer than your standard dividing. The one on the correct edge is the best model here.

(For the conscientious among you; indeed, you are correct, I didn't join throughout the entire the corner to corner lines prior to sewing this wave area :-)

Sashiko is pardoning. Numerous inconsistencies will vanish in the in general completed sewed plan, yet here are a couple of things that will leap out in the completed piece, which you will need to evade:

o   stitches that are abnormally long or exceptionally short (contrasted with the remainder of your fastens),

o   stitches that get into another fasten,

o   stitches that run into crossing points or past the line they are meeting

o   stitches in places that ought to be vacant, similar to the focal point of flax leaf plans.

The following is an illustration of sashiko join meeting yet not entering a convergence

Other than that, little varieties in your sewing they will simply add to the uniqueness.

Bit by bit Guide to Sashiko Stitching

Here and there I need to complete a task super quick, however recently I have gotten a hand sewing project when I need to loosen up. The lethargic, thoughtful cycle of shaping each fasten in turn is quieting. Sashiko is an ideal procedure for those occasions. It's simple, versatile and requires only a couple supplies. Undertakings can be any size, from napkins on up.

Sashiko is a Japanese society create that is many years old with establishes in reasonableness. Since ranchers required comfortable dress that would last, the ladies (typically) sewed layers of texture together to add warmth and to fix worn zones. Texture colored dim blue with indigo, when matched with unbleached cream string, given a range to innovatively communicating realistic plans. Humble work garments became masterpieces with join.

Sashiko signifies "little wounds", and that impeccably depicts the line. It's a running join that wounds the texture back to front and back once more. Ideal line size? Consider grains rice. My fastens are more similar to long-grain rice – not exactly conventional – ha!

Today, Sashiko strings and textures arrive in a rainbow of tones, so your ventures can go with anything you pick. My undertaking has dark texture and green string – not customary by any means! On the off chance that you would prefer not to stamp your pattern, you can buy pre-printed Sashiko boards. In the event that you join the ran lines, you can become acclimated to the vibe of even fastens. At that point the imprints wash away. Nobody will know!

Bit by bit Sashiko

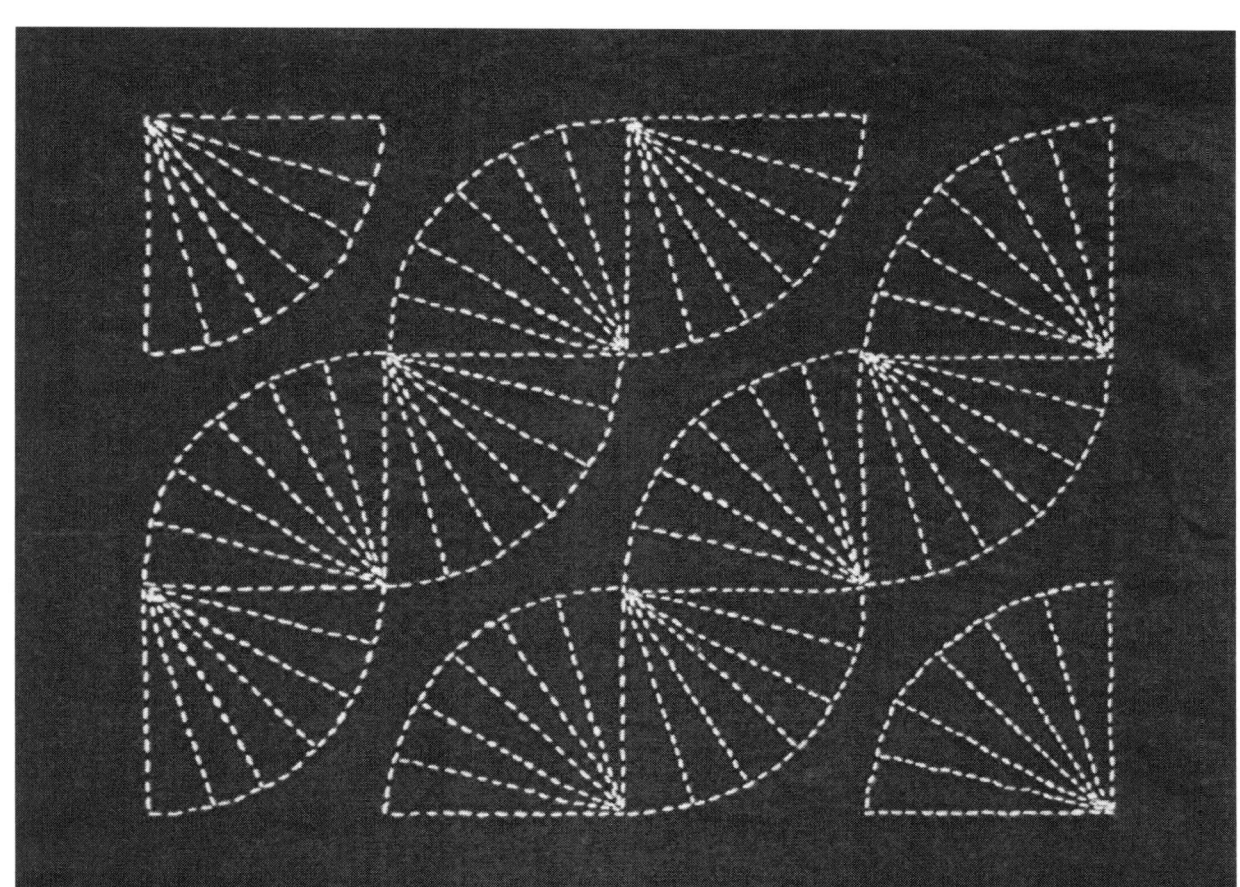

- Marking your texture for Sashiko

- Selecting your texture for Sashiko

- Sashiko sewing plans

- FREE downloadable pattern in two sizes

- Transferring your Sashiko plan to texture

- Choosing your string for Sashiko sewing

- Selecting the correct needle for Sashiko sewing

- Tips for working with customary Sashiko string

- Stitching your Sashiko pattern on texture

How about we begin! Except if you chose a pre-printed board, you will need to check your picked pattern onto texture. There are heaps of alternatives out there, beyond what I can show here, and each has its benefits and weaknesses. So make a few inquiries and test, test, test!

Denoting your texture for Sashiko

A Hera Marker is a negligibly intrusive stamping alternative. You never need to hone or top off, so it's consistently all set. You draw your line by squeezing the sharp edge of the device as you "draw" on the texture. It leaves a wrinkled line for you to follow with fastens. No deleting required! You will need great lighting in the event that you pick this technique, as the imprints can be inconspicuous.

One of my go-to decisions for checking on dull textures is the Clover White Marking Pen. It works like a straightforward ballpoint pen, yet the "ink" comes out clear and becomes white as it dries. The imprints wash out with water or the hint of a hot iron. The scarcely discernible differences are incredible for multifaceted plans, and the point follows the edge of format precisely. In any case, don't leave your piece in a hot vehicle. Your imprints may vanish.

The Hemline Water Erasable Pencil is a mechanical pencil, which I like since I can't monitor my sharpener. I utilized white for this model on dark texture, however it additionally comes in blue to use on light textures. It leaves dependable imprints that you can eliminate with water.

This is the thing that I at last utilized for this task: Miracle Chalk. It comes in this present tailor's chalk style and in a pudgy colored pencil design. It floats over the texture, so following my plan went rapidly. I wanted to fasten in the nights, so the strong line with high difference was a genuine benefit for me. The imprints stay clear from the beginning of the undertaking to the completion, at that point vanish totally with a hot iron. Or on the other hand when left in a hot vehicle – see above.

Choosing your texture for Sashiko sewing

Early Sashiko was sewed on indigo-colored hemp fabric, and you could possibly discover it in niche stores. Yet, the majority of the present Sashiko stitchers join on medium weight, approximately woven cotton, material or cotton/cloth mix. The weave is significant – knitting cottons (particularly batiks) are excessively firmly woven to work with heaver strings and needles. They may show openings and puckering. Go exemplary with blue, or fasten on another shading that fulfills you

Choosing plans for your Sashiko sewing

Sashiko plans, even those with breathtaking components, are regularly founded on a basic matrix. Achieved stitchers can draw simply a network on the texture and fill in the plan by eye, essentially sewing from one corner to another. The majority of us, notwithstanding, need a pattern. With Sashiko's rich custom, there are incalculable choices. You can plan your own pattern or search for books and patterns from sashiko craftsmen.

Moving your Sashiko plan to texture

I love my light box! It permits me to see everything about following a plan, and it's a great deal more easy to use than taping paper to a window, particularly on the off chance that you need to follow when the sun isn't sparkling. (Or then again you would prefer not to move that seat close to the sunniest window far removed.) As you can see, I selected to print additional intense and dull lines for the most noteworthy perceivability.

I didn't know the pattern would show for following on dark texture, however here it is! The texture is Essex by Robert Kaufman, a similar cotton material mix presented previously. This is generous texture, not a shaky low-string tally open weave, and the pattern is still clear. Presently, to stamp!

Here is the task in measure, showing the Miracle Chalk checks up until now. With paper impeding the light on piece of the piece, you can see the distinction and how obviously the imprints show up. It's a decent stunt to mind your advancement – did I get every one of the spines of that fan?

The checking is done, and it's an ideal opportunity to begin sewing. I will join simply the fans, not the line portions between fans. Those will help me keep the venture square and vanish when I eliminate different imprints.

Picking string for your Sashiko sewing

You have options with regards to string. Conventional Sashiko cotton string has a delicate contort that is exquisite to work with. It goes ahead skeins, which require some planning before you start to line, yet it's not difficult to do. In the event that you need to go this conventional course, Sashiko string is accessible in an enticing exhibit of tones.

Perle cotton is another alternative for Sashiko sewing. Size 8 is comparable in weight to the conventional strings, however with a marginally more tight bend. Contingent upon the brand, you may see it on skeins or spooled into balls. Loads of tones and simple to discover!

Choosing needles for your Sashiko sewing

You will require needles. Yet, an extraordinary needles. Sashiko needles truly are the awesome, with the developing fame of the specialty, they are a lot simpler to discover. These needles are longer than other weaving needles, so you can stack more fastens on the needle prior to getting it through the texture. Since the string makes less goes through the texture, the more drawn out needle decreases grating and keeps the string from fraying.

Tips for working with conventional Sashiko string

I utilized Sashiko string for my undertaking, yet first I needed to prepare the string for sewing. It's only a couple steps and results in string that is sans tangle and pre-sliced to the ideal length. To begin with, delicately slide off the paper covering. Make an effort not to upset the strings. Keep the skein similarly all things considered. You will unfurl the skein in the subsequent stage.

Track down the little bunch that ties the strings together. Do this tenderly, without upsetting the skein. Tip: When the skein emerges from the bundle, it is collapsed in thirds, so you may have better karma finding the bunch by contact instead of by sight. The bunch might be inside an overlay. Try not to open up the folds until you have found the bunch!

When you have the bunch, delicately bother the skein into a huge clean circle.

Presently you can discover one finish of string (it probably won't be close to the bunch) and cut two pieces, each around 5 inches in length.

Wrap one of your string portions around the string where the bunch holds the entwine. You need this to be cozy, yet not tight. You will get strings through this circle each in turn for sewing.

On the contrary side from the bunch, slice through the whole circle of string. The length of the cut strings you have quite recently made is the ideal length for sewing.

Stitching your Sashiko pattern onto fabric

Some persons when stitching knot the ends of their thread before stitching.. But I think it's worth it to keep the stitching smooth and not risk having a knot pop through to the front of the work.

I begin by bringing the thread up 3 or 4 stitches from the beginning of my stitching line, leaving a 1 to 2 inch tail. The stitches should be about 1-1/2 times longer on the front than on the back, so check both sides so you can be consistent going forward. Then I stitch back towards the beginning of my pattern line, ending with a "down" stitch.

This view from the back shows the unknotted thread tail and the back of the first stitches. Note that from the back, the stitches are shorter – that's as it should be. Tension should be relaxed, but not "loopy". If your fabric shows any puckers, give another tug to make a smooth stitch line.

Now, reverse direction and pass the needle BETWEEN the back of each stitch and the fabric. Tip: Make these passes leading with the threaded eye of the needle. This will prevent snags on your previous stitches or the fabric. Then insert the needle one stitch length from the thread tail, but don't pull it through yet.

Check the front of your work to ensure that the needle exits where you want it to on the pattern line. This point is the beginning of the next stitch and will be a seamless continuation of your pattern. So adjust now, if needed, then pull the thread through.

Continue stitching, either one stitch at a time or loading several stitches on the needle before pulling through. Be aware of tension. I tend to be a "tight" stitcher, which is good for some things, but not for Sashiko! So I give the fabric a little tug after each series of stitches to prevent puckers.

When you come to a corner or a sharp turn, one stitch should begin or end at the apex. This keeps the appearance sharp. Don't pull too tightly!

If you leave a small loop on the back between corner stitches, it will prevent puckers and keep your work smooth on the front.

When you feel comfortable and get on a roll, try loading several stitches on the needle before pulling the stitches through. On a straight line, you can load more stitches at once to speed up your work. Give the fabric a gentle tug to relax the thread.

On curves, load fewer stitches at a time.

If you need to begin a new line of the pattern and that starting point is no more than an inch or so away, travel to the next starting point by making a loose loop on the back. Here, I have stitched around the outside of the fan back to my starting point and need to travel to start stitching the spines. Insert the needle where the next line of stitching will begin.

Continue stitching along your marked pattern lines.

When you need to "tie off" the end of your thread, weave it back through a few stitches on the wrong side of your work. Trim thread, leaving a 1 to 2 inch tail. Begin the new thread just as you did when you began stitching.

Now you know what to do! Enjoy your stitching experience, knowing that you can steal a moment to get in a few stitches or have a nice, long, slow-stitching personal retreat.

Here is the first fan all stitched!

It's easier to see the design with the pattern lines removed.

When my stitching was complete, I pressed from the wrong side to avoid flattening the stitches too much or pressing a sheen onto the threads. I like the nod to tradition with a dark background and light thread. But the zingy contrast of bright green on black adds a touch of fun. I think this might be a throw pillow when it grows up!

END

[1]

Made in United States
Troutdale, OR
09/06/2024

22631410R00064